DATE DUE

MY 28'00			
MY 31 00			
DE 19 08			

DEMCO 38-296

GARLAND STUDIES ON

THE ELDERLY IN AMERICA

edited by

STUART BRUCHEY
ALLAN NEVINS PROFESSOR EMERITUS
COLUMBIA UNIVERSITY

A GARLAND SERIES

PHYSICIANS' ATTITUDES TOWARD ELDER SUICIDE

LORI M. SECOULER

GARLAND PUBLISHING, Inc.
A MEMBER OF THE TAYLOR & FRANCIS GROUP
NEW YORK & LONDON / 1998

g-in-Publication Data

Secouler, Lori M., 1942–
     Physicians' attitudes toward elder suicide / Lori M. Secouler.
        p.   cm. — (Garland studies on the Elderly in America)
     Includes bibliographical references and index.
     ISBN 0-8153-3005-7 (alk. paper)
     1. Aged—Suicidal behavior. 2. Aged—Suicidal behavior—
United States. 3. Aged—Suicidal behavior—United States—Public
opinion. 4. Physicians (General practice)—United States—Attitudes. 5. Public opinion—United States. I. Title. II. Series.
HV6545.2.S43 1997
362.28'084'6—dc21

                                                       97-32973

Printed on acid-free, 250-year-life paper
Manufactured in the United States of America

Contents

Preface

While working in the field of geriatric psychology, I found it difficult to avoid the constant barrage of media attention on the ever increasing problem of "assisted suicide." More and more people were helping others to end their lives—and making their pain public. The main questions that need answering are being answered by the public and not the physicians caring for the elderly. It is my belief that these questions must be addressed by both groups. These medico-legal and philosophical arguments encompass such fundamental queries such as: Is the elderly patient mentally unstable due to pain . . . or the stress of looming dependency? What comprises a "rational" suicide? Who can make the final decision about mental stability? Pronouncements, tenets and views regarding voluntary death have been passed from religion to medicine to psychiatry, bioethics and back. This study was undertaken for those who are preparing for, or confused by, the changes that are already taking place in the public arena by individuals, organizations and various state legislative bodies with regard to the legalization of physician assisted suicide. The pilot study is a very preliminary exploration of suburban physicians' attitudes which will hopefully allow us to begin to understand the concerns of those with the capability of helping to make death, as well as life, a integral part of common medical practice and training.

Much anecdotal material is available regarding physicians' beliefs about elder suicide, and suicide in general, but there is no research available that looks at family practice physicians' attitudes (toward elder suicide) as a group. It is the group, and not the individual physician, that has the power to effect policy. As the *Epilogue* of this work states,

The American Geriatrics Society in 1996, and the Supreme Court in 1997, have begun to address these issues on a legislative level. However, we need to continue to investigate those who are our first line of defense; our local family physicians and the pressures placed on them by our aging population. Historical material is available from many sources with regard to suicide beliefs, and many people are writing about the problems of the elderly. The attitudes of mental health professionals, as well as ethicists and the elderly themselves, have been elucidated, and are important in our quest for reason. In combining these areas of concern and progress into one book, I feel that we will have a better understanding of the dilemma our society is facing at this moment, and what we need to do to prepare for the future.

Acknowledgments

To my fiancé, John Lukatchik, who continually encouraged me to pursue my goal, even though it meant that I would be physically two thousand miles away from home for what seemed to be an eternity . . . and mentally on another planet the rest of the time—Thank you for being there when I needed you.

To my sons, Ian and Adam, who often did without a mother's touch—Thank you for being so patient.

To my Union Institute committee: Bill McKelvie, Linda Hopkins, Pam Tronetti, Tony Glascock, Dorothy Kulp and Allen Miller—Thank you for continually pushing me to strive for excellence, and for reminding me that I could really contribute something important and unique.

To Mirca Liberti and Louise Fradkin, co-founders of Children of Aging Parents—Thank you for giving me a focus and chance to help others.

Physicians' Attitudes toward Elder Suicide

I

The Problem of Elder Suicide

Suicide, the choice of death over life, is a phenomenon that is found at all age levels from childhood to old age, for both genders, for all ethnic groups, and at all levels of the socioeconomic strata. However, the pattern is that suicide rates increase with age, and this can be observed in every country where statistics are maintained. In comparison to other age groups, the elderly are more serious about killing themselves, and more successful in their attempts. (For the purpose of this work, I am considering the age of 65 as the beginning of elderhood, since most bureaucratic systems in the United States have created and enforced this delineation.)

Statistics compiled by the National Center for Health Statistics show that the U.S. suicide rate for people aged 65 or older rose 25% between 1981 and 1986 to a rate of 21.6 per 100,000. In the same period, the overall national rate rose 5% to 12.8 per 100,000. (Science News:1989). The suicide rate (among elderly age groupings) for elderly white males increased from 41.1 in 1970 to 45.0 per 100,000 in 1988. (US Bureau of Census, 1991, p. 86)

Taking into consideration that many elderly suicides are not reported because of family stigma, insurance benefits, and the common practice of certifying an older person's death as accidental or natural, the number of unreported suicides may be as great as the number of reported suicides. (Miller, 1978, p. 2) At this time, over half of all single occupant car crash fatalities involving elderly men are now being viewed as suspected suicides. (Personal communication from Geriatrician, P. Tronetti, D.O., May 1989, and also confirmed by the Pennsylvania State Police Special Investigations Team.) Termed "autocide" by Evans and Farberow, forensic experts and highway safety officials report that these fatal "accidents" are probably deliberate in one-fourth of reported cases. Statistics for the elderly population are unavailable at this time. (Evans & Farberow, 1988, p. 26)

Suicide rates for both genders increase with chronological age until about the 24th year of life. The female suicide rate continues to increase until the mid-forties and then declines through the mid-eighties. (National statistics usually do not go beyond this age category.) The male suicide rate rises and dips between 25 and 40, keeping well above the rate for females, and then becomes increasingly frequent with age until the 80's. In the 75-79 age range, for example, there are 42.5 male suicides per 100,000 as compared with 7.5 for females. (Birren & Schaie, 1985, pp. 634-636). Statistics for those over 65 show that the suicide rate in 1988 for white males was nearly four times the national average (45.0 deaths in 100,000), three times the rate for older black men, six times the rate for older white women, and 26 times that of older black women. (Statistical Abstract, 1991, P. 86) At the time of the publication of this monograph, several other authors have added their statistics to this ongoing problem. Yeates Conwell in his study for the American Foundation for Suicide Prevention (1996) and John McIntosh (McIntosh, Santos, Hubbard and Overholser, 1996) both state that between 6,000 and 6,300 older adults take their own lives each year. According to Conwell, "Among the elderly, suicide is the thirteenth leading cause of death;" and McIntosh states that ". . . nearly 18 older Americans kill themselves each day." It must be noted that to date, all writings and research regarding the demographics of elder death continue to reiterate the material in this study. On a more human level, data from the latest government statistics on suicide (from Deaths by Selected Causes, 1993, p. 95) is shown in thousands rather than hundred thousands, making each deliberate death even more poignant.

According to Pokorny (in Zarit, 1980, p. 227), women make more suicide attempts than men, but men of any age are more likely to complete the act. Among the elderly, half of all elderly persons attempting suicide are successful. "Passive suicides," such as when a person refuses food or fails to maintain a therapeutic drug regimen, is most probably underestimated and, therefore, the overall numbers of successful attempts are, in reality, higher. (Assisted suicides and other forms of "elected death" {my term} will be discussed in Chapters 3 and 5.) One reason for the high completion rate is that the older suicide is not as likely to intend that his or her actions have manipulative or negative affect on another person. When the suicide is not intended to directly affect someone, the attempt is likely to be more dangerous. (Dorpat & Boswell in Zarit, 1980, p. 227) Elderly people contemplating suicide also show much less ambivalence and are less likely to be rescued from their suicidal activities. (Miller, 1979: pp. 1, 23)

In order to intervene appropriately, clinicians must be aware of the hidden clues that patients exhibit, since at least 75% of suicides have visited a physician "shortly before their fatal acts" and showed no apparent suicidal behavior, such as reporting intent or requesting an inordinate amount of potentially lethal medication. (Barraclough in Miller, 1979, p. 69) Other researchers have reported that at least 10% of all suicides in the United States consult a physician on the actual day of their self-inflicted deaths. (Rockwell & O'Brien in Miller, 1979, p. 69)

This leads to the assumption that not only is suicide prevention underemphasized in primary medical and continuing medical education, it may be even more neglected with regard to the elderly. In 1992, according to the research branch of the Philadelphia Geriatric Center, one of the foremost training institutions in the U.S., the medical specialists concerned with the elderly (geriatrician) numbered only in the hundreds in the U.S. . . . and Geropsychologists had, and still have, an even smaller cadre. By 1996, the number of certified aging specialists had increased to approximately 6,784. This cadre includes those in internal medicine, family practice and psychiatry. However, according to a report by the Alliance for Aging Research, at least 20,000 physicians with geriatrics training are needed to provide appropriate care for the current population of over 30 million older citizens. The Alliance (AAR) calculates a deficit of over 16,000 professionals in academia, primary practice and consultative situations. (Fanning, 1996) These specialists may be aware of the problem, but they are not always in a position to teach others, or to convince them that an older person's decision to commit suicide may encompass more than a result of clinical depression or other mental illness. This leaves the general practitioner at a disadvantage; if there is no preparation for an aging clientele at the scholastic level for the average medical student going into general practice, personal biases and beliefs about aging (indirectly influencing attitudes toward elder suicide) may not be challenged. (Please see Chapter VI for a discussion of the American Geriatric Society's views regarding Physician Assisted Suicide.)

The original purpose of this study was to highlight and investigate those biases and beliefs—the attitudes of a specific group of general practitioners toward elder suicide. My working hypothesis was that general practitioners treat elderly patients differently than other age groups with respect to suicide due to a perceived qualitative difference in an older person's choosing death over life. The attitudes espoused by the physicians regarding elder suicide gives us a view of the care that our medical profession delivers to the elderly and how this care may be based on personal beliefs about aging, rather than didactic studies or empirical experience.

In order to study these attitudes, we must look at the historical underpinnings that create and enforce belief systems, and we must not neglect those forces that impinge on medical practice, such as limited resources in an aging society and the health care system that promotes technology for its own sake (ie: the machine exists, therefore, we must use it). We must also be aware of the cultural norms that appear to contribute to elder suicide—the ageism that exists despite all of our supposedly enlightened treatment of those who are no longer "young." Perhaps by focusing on the myriad facets of ageism that crystalize into externalized behavior and internalized grief, we can begin to aid the professional caregiver in his or her quest for fair and humane treatment of the elderly.

Table 1: Total* Suicide Rates By Age Group: 1970 To 1988

Age	1970	1980	1988
ALL AGES**	1.6	11.9	12.4
10-14 Yrs.	0.6	0.8	1.4
15-18 Yrs.	5.9	8.5	11.3
20-24 Yrs.	12.2	16.1	15.0
25-34 Yrs.	14.1	16.0	15.4
35-44 Yrs.	16.9	15.4	14.8
45-54 Yrs.	20.0	15.9	14.6
55-64 Yrs.	21.4	15.9	15.6
65 Yrs. & Over	20.8	17.8	21.0
65-74 Yrs.	20.8	16.9	18.4
75-84 Yrs.	21.2	19.1	25.9
85 Yrs. & Over	19.0	19.2	20.5

*Includes other races not shown below.

** Includes other age groups not shown.

All figures are based on rate per 100,000 population

Source: US Bureau of the Census, *Statistical Abstract of the United States: 1991,* 111th ed. Washington DC:1991

Table 2: Elder Suicide By Age Group, Gender And Race

White Males	1970	1980	1988
65 yrs. & over	41.1	37.5	45.0
65-74 yrs.	38.7	32.5	35.4
75-84 yrs.	45.5	45.5	61.5
85 yrs. & over	45.8	52.8	65.8

White Females	1970	1980	1988
65 yrs. & over	8.5	6.5	7.1
65-74 yrs.	9.6	7.0	7.3
75-84 yrs.	7.2	5.7	7.4
85 yrs. & over	5.8	5.8	5.3

Black Males	1970	1980	1988
65 yrs. & over	8.7	11.4	14.0
65-74 yrs.	8.7	11.1	12.9
75-84 yrs.	8.9	10.5	17.6
85 yrs. & over	8.7	18.9	10.0

Black Females	1970	1980	1988
65 yrs. & over	2.6	1.4	1.6
65-74 yrs.	2.9	1.7	2.0
75-84 yrs.	1.7	1.4	1.3
85 yrs. & over	2.8	—	—

All figures are based on rate per 100,000 population
Source: US Bureau of the Census, *Statistical Abstract of the United States: 1991,* 111th ed. Washington DC:1991

Table 3: Abstracted from "Deaths by Selected Causes and Characteristics, 1993 (in thousands)

Age, Sex & Race	Total Deaths all causes	Suicide
Both Sexes Total	2,268.6	31.1
65 to 74 years old		3.0
75 to 84 years old		2.4
85 years or older		0.8
Males, Total	1,161.8	25.0
65 to 74 years old		2.4
75 to 84 years old		2.0
85 years and older		0.6
Females, Total	1,106.8	6.1
65 to 74 years old		0.6
75 to 84 years old		0.4
85 years and older		0.1
White, Both Sexes	1,951.4	28.0
65 to 74 years old		2.9
75 to 84 years old		2.3
85 years and older		0.8
Black, Both Sexes	282.2	2.3
65 to 74 years old		0.1
75 to 84 years old		0.1
85 years and older		Z

Z=fewer than 50. All totals may include deaths with age not stated. Source: U.S. National Center for Health Statistics, Vital Statistics of the United States, Annual.

II
Factors Contributing to Elder Suicide

DEFINITIONS OF AGEISM

Age prejudice, or ageism, is a dislike of aging and older people based on the belief that aging makes people less employable, potentially demented, unattractive, and asexual. (Atchley, 1980, p. 261) Comfort defines ageism as ". . . the notion that people cease to be people, cease to be the same people or become people of a distinct and inferior kind, by virtue of having lived a specified number of years." (Comfort, 1976, p. 35) Robert Butler, the first to use the term "ageism" adds a more personal note to the phenomena when he states that " . . . ageism serves a highly personal objective, protecting younger (usually middle aged) individuals--often at high emotional cost-from thinking about things they fear (aging, illness, death)." (Butler, 1975, P. 12)

THE HISTORICAL ROOTS OF AGEISM

Myths About the Past

Most of us have heard about the "good old days" in America when the elderly were respected just because they were old, and knowledge accumulated through life experience was always respectfully heeded. Unhappily, the "good old days" never really existed, and there was only a very short period in the life of the United States when age and sagacity were counted as linked traits; Colonial America before 1790.

American attitudes toward the elderly, and aging itself, have continually changed throughout our relatively short history. According to Fischer (1978, p. 85), "The pattern of change itself, was changed sometime between 1790 and 1850." Previous patterns of slow social variation gave way to permutation, a change in the basic order of social hierarchy. Before 1790, the median age was 16 years. Anyone who made it to elderhood, reportedly less than 2% of the population (1978, p. 3), was accorded high status, especially if the person was male, and had a livelihood. In meetinghouses all over New England, elders were ranked by age, wealth, power, race and gender. Among all the many distinctions detailed by Fischer, none was more important than age. (1978, pp. 38-40, 78-79) The year 1790 is seen as pivotal in age relations because it was the end of the *ancien regime*, a world run by old and powerful institutions, headed by old and powerful men. The costumes, inheritance laws, language and social mores reflected a veneration of the powerful elderly. White wigs were worn to mimic elder wisdom (Charles & DeAnfransio, 1970, pp. 118-127), and paunch-like vestments showed the world that one was not only old but well fed. (Kybalova et al, 1968, pp. 189-221) Not much mention was made of the elder poor. Most did not survive long enough to be a burden, and if they did, they were usually treated as classless beggars. (Fischer, 1978, pp. 60-63) Haber has noted that even before the social revolutionary period of the late 1700's, scores of elderly persons no longer possessed the means of integrating themselves into society. These were the men and women who lacked strong ties to family, occupation and property. In many ways, this was a foretaste of aging in the nineteenth and twentieth centuries, since the same factors tend to shape the nature of old age in this society.

> The retired, the childless, the widowed, and the poor often found themselves segregated from society in their last years. Few bonds existed to define their roles or solidify their status. Without these links, the prestige and power of old age disappeared. (Haber, 1985, p. 17)

Post Revolutionary Attitudes

After 1790, many meeting houses, the religious focal point of social status, changed their seating patterns to reflect wealth and political placement; people stopped powdering their hair; the rights of primogeniture (inheritance by the first born male) were changed to placate a growing body of landless young men; and language began to reflect a harsher climate for the American over 60. Pejorative words for old women were always in use, but now the elderly male was a target. For example, the term "fogy" meant a wounded military veteran in the vocabulary of the early 1700's; by 1800, it became a disrespectful name for an old man. (Fischer, 1978, pp. 86-99)

The American and French Revolutions, in doing away with the *ancien regime*, had changed the way the elderly were seen and treated. The subsequent increased longevity due to more peaceful revolutions in medical care and sanitation, creating the modern dilemma of resource management in an aging society, added to the negative view of elderhood in America.

SELF-ATTITUDES OF THE ELDERLY

The complicity between the elderly person and the "ageists" is activated by this nation's proported "beliefs" regarding personal independence, rather than a more humanistic interdependence. Zest and enthusiasm are prized, rather than cautious deliberation. Agility and speed, the hallmarks of youthfulness, are the predominant values, not to mention physical beauty. These values hold for the world of work and in all areas of the social order. Erik Erikson finds that it is not surprising that ageism poses a tremendous problem for many older people, and the cruelest aspect of this cultural attitude is older people's vulnerability to stereotype. Stereotyping is deeply ingrained in our culture and our economy.

> After all, we throw old things away-they are too difficult to mend. New ones are more desirable and up-to-date, incorporating the latest know-how. Old things are obsolete, valueless, and disposable. (Erikson, et al, 1986, p. 301)

Old people have been socially labeled as incompetent for a very long period in many industrialized nations. Their lives are defined by the paradigm of middle age . . . the time when they were expected to be most productive. If our social world tells us we are handicapped and/or incompetent, no longer relevant in our beliefs, skills or productivity, we begin to act as if it were true. Old people, as has been mentioned before, accept and comply with the stereotypes, label each other as "Old Fogies" and reduce their social horizons because they do not want to be with "old people" (who may possibly be of the same age [1]).

Many people who have accepted the label of incompetent, use it as an excuse for a multiplicity of reasons. "What do you expect, *he's old,*" is now transformed into "What do you expect, *I'm old.*"

Fear of humiliation, being told that they are too old to do something competently, or to look acceptable, may keep the average elderly person from attacking that label. The shock of suddenly finding oneself a member of a group that is considered superannuated (too old to be included in the original group) may produce this fear. For many, this is a trauma that is never healed. They have accepted society's image, because it hurts less than dealing with possible failure, and because there is protection in numbers. Instead of rejecting the negative image, many older people band together, choosing not even to socialize with other age groups at all, to protect themselves from possible social rejection. They isolate themselves to create a new role, one that younger people do not find threatening; the role of "senior citizen."

THE LOSS OF RELEVANT ROLES

Aside from the decrease in social radius through death or migration, ageism may express itself in role loss. The roles that society ascribes to its members, such as "productive worker" have now become very vague. The loss of peers who provide social support and role models, and the loss of social roles, added to the vague norms that are prescribed to those of a "certain age," may be termed "preconditions of susceptibility" for depression and humiliation. Atchley states that the trend of these role losses or changes

> . . . is from roles that are mainly general to roles that are mainly specific. For example, people may leave a job role through retirement and cope with this change by increasing the time they spend in specific relationships. (Atchley, 1980, p.71)

General roles have widely known norms, ie: being male, while specific roles cannot be well defined outside of their particular context. Anticipatory socialization, the process of learning the rules regarding a position one will occupy in the future, is a problem for the elderly because of the aforementioned vague norms, and as a result, the older person often has to negotiate the rights and duties of this new position with the very people whose attitudes toward aging are negative.

PROBLEMS OF AGING FOR MALES

Elderly males in the United States have a much harder time dealing with the aging process, due in part, to the kinds of roles they have played in society. (Atchley, 1980: pp. 171-178) The roles, for most, would be "productive worker" and "breadwinner" with little time left for husbanding and parenting. Erving Goffman, in writing about stigmatized individuals, increases our understanding of social utility when we look at the plight of elderly men who have defined themselves through their work, have few coping skills outside of industry, and are humiliated by their perceived uselessness. Goffman quotes an unemployed worker during the Depression: "How hard and humiliating it is to bear the name of an unemployed man. When I go out, I cast down my eyes because I feel myself wholly inferior. . . ." (Goffman, 1963, p. 17) Humiliation, for elderly American males, is tied more to the Puritan work ethic than any other aspect of aging. It is important to understand that retirement, forced or voluntary, changes more than finances and gender roles. The unemployed man is often deemed incompetent, loses autonomy at work and in the home, and has an impaired self image as a result. This loss of autonomy comes at a time when other losses, such as the death of a spouse or significant others, have already begun to weaken those who lack adequate coping skills. The proverbial "gold watch" does nothing to ameliorate the painful realization that one has been deemed expendable by those who are a primary source of validation. Comfort calls retirement ". . . another name for dismissal and unemployment. It must be prepared for exactly as you would prepare for dismissal and unemployment." (Comfort,1976, p. 29)

PROBLEMS OF AGING FOR FEMALES

Growing older is a problem for both genders, but appearing older is especially hard for females. Melamed equates "appearance anxiety" in elderly women to "performance anxiety" in men. (Melamed, 1983, pp.

69-70) The loss of self-esteem experienced because one is no longer a candidate for Miss, or even Mrs. America, is due in part to our society's emphasis on what constitutes a rating of "10." Women have been judged on looks, rather than accomplishment, for so long that recent raising of consciousness for both genders has not been effective in eradicating this problem for many older women. If one has spent 60 years trying to match the American ideal, it will take a long time to create a different, more personal "ideal." The cliché says that beauty is in the eye of the beholder . . . the problem is that the beholder most often is a self-judge, due to the past lack of positive role models for a handsome old age, and a lack of interested older men.

Older women are often considered genderless . . . neutered by age. Freud, in an article on obsessional neurosis writes:

> It is well known, and has been a matter for much complaint, that women often alter strangely in character after they have abandoned their genital functions. They become quarrelsome, peevish, and argumentative, petty and miserly; in fact they display sadistic and anal-erotic traits which were not theirs in the era of womanliness. (Freud in Strachey, 1959, pp. 2, 130)

More recently, one of the popular psychological gurus wrote in his best seller, *Everything You Wanted to Know About Sex*, the following statement:

> As the estrogen is shut off, a women comes as close as she can to being a man. Increased facial hair, deepened voice, obesity and the decline of breasts and female genitalia all contribute to a masculine appearance. Coarsened features, enlargement of the clitoris, and gradual baldness complete the tragic picture. Not really a man but no longer a functional woman, these individuals live in the world of intersex. (Reuben in Melamed, p. 93)

If the so-called experts are perpetuating the denigration of older women, and it is reinforced by countless years of anti-female bias and stereotyping of beauty, we well might wonder how any woman escapes humiliation or rises above this intimate grief.

BEREAVEMENT

The loss of a spouse, especially in a long-term marriage, has a particularly devastating effect on elderly women. Many clinicians working with women suffering from abnormally long bereavements have come to believe that widowhood can be a terminal disease. Many older women have never written a check, made a major purchase in their own name without male counsel, handled investments . . . or even attended social functions without the ever-present spouse. For a working-class widow, not only are the decision-making processes undeveloped, there is self doubt with regard to ever being able to function efficiently.

Older men also have a difficult time with bereavement, but research has shown that widowers have better economic resources and a better chance for remarriage than widows due to work related income and pension plans, and the over-abundance of available older women. (Atchley, 1980, pp. 207-216) The widower who finds it difficult to cook and clean for himself is more likely to find willing helpers than a widow trying to make sense of financial strategies, or regain a social life. A widow is often considered a threat to friends with living spouses; she is apt to be left out of former group pursuits. The widower is more warmly welcomed because he is not perceived as a threat; he is often pampered by these same women who sense a need for nurturing. (Melamed, 1983)

PHYSICAL AGING

The physical aspects of the aging process can be potentially humiliating, and may contribute to lethal, self-injurious behavior. In the recent past, the loss of visual acuity was very troubling to those of middle age and older. The optical lens industry and new surgery techniques have taken many visual problems out of the category of "uncorrectable sensory decline due to aging." Hearing loss, on the other hand, is still very much felt by those over 65 as an admission of decrepitude. Hearing aides are often shunned, even when they are the expensive, miniscule devices worn by elder statesmen. Many elderly with bladder problems have rejected the humiliation of wearing adult "diapers" and have elected to isolate themselves instead; medical help is often unsought due to embarrassment or the conviction that nothing can be done for the condition. Advertisements for adult "diaper" products have perpetuated the myth that incontinence is a normal by-product of aging, and only the tiny print at the bottom of the television screen mentions the possibility of medical intervention.

The fear of memory loss in the elderly has created problems for those who equate youth with total recall. It is normal to lose some short-term memory as one ages, and it may only be due to the tremendous amount of information processed, and not mental frailty. (Poon in Birren & Schaie, 1985, pp. 435-437).

The loss of the faculties needed to operate a motor vehicle may not be noticed, except by frightened caregivers, and by accidents that were avoidable given a fairly normal response time for decision making. Elderly males, some of whom have driven for seventy years, consider driving a right and not a privilege granted by the state. The loss of that license to drive not only engenders humiliation due to loss of "manhood," but increases isolation and dependency. Many of our older women considered driving something special, a man's domain, and though the loss of her license limits her independence, she does not usually feel it as a loss of what it means to be a woman.

PSYCHOLOGICAL CONCERNS

Responses to external life strains that serve to prevent, avoid or control emotional distress, ie: coping skills that are developed during adolescence and adulthood, are seen as a function of whether an older person succumbs to a suicidal crisis. Black and white females are seen to have developed more varied coping skills outside of the workplace, while the coping skills that males have developed do not as readily carry over into retirement. (Secouler, 1988, p. 3) Busse and Pfeiffer (1969: pp. 212-213, 221-224) note that individuals who have been able to develop trusting relationships with others, a clearly defined and valued identity, a sense of personal autonomy, who have previously faced adversity without succumbing to it, and who have performed satisfactorily in marriage and in work make the best adjustment in later life. On the other hand, Miller (1979: pp. 10-11), Batchelor and Napier (1953, pp. 1186-1190) and Birren (1964: pp. 258-260)) have all found that a significantly greater percentage of people who had committed suicide had come from a "broken home" or been raised by domineering, critical and insensitive parents. There was also a high incidence of mental illness in these families. Personality characteristics such as shyness, undue sensitivity, dependency, anxiety and hypochondriasis hamper the development of close interpersonal relationships, and in later life produces an "at risk" elder. Those who have used alcohol as a means to cope with problems are considered by most as more likely to choose suicide as a solution.

The aforementioned lack of early acquired coping skills in the elderly has been linked to an increase in clinical depression. Clinical depression is associated with increased alcohol consumption (with or without previous use as a coping mechanism), physical pain and any number of distressing symptoms, the worst of which is suicidal ideation. (Zarit, 1980, pp. 227-233) It should be noted that the majority of these elder suicides do not have a terminal illness or suffer intractable physical pain. (Secouler & Tronetti, 1989, pp. 21-24) According to Osgood, elderly widowers represent the most "at risk" group for suicide. (1985, pp. xx-xxii)

INSTITUTIONAL FACTORS

As most of us are unhappily aware, hospitals and other facilities, especially long term care entities, are what Goffman called "total institutions," within which the "inmates" live out all aspects of their lives. Robert E. Murphy, an anthropologist suffering from decreasing mobility due to a spinal chord tumor, reminds us in his book, *The Body Silent* (1987, pp. 19-22) that the truly closed off institution ". . . generally tries to expunge prior identities and to make the individual assume one that is imposed on him by authority." The role loss that our elderly experience is further exacerbated when they are chronically ill. He or she is shorn of all other social roles and is regarded as one sick body among many. There are definite social skills in illness: the good patient makes no complaints, waits interminably for attention, and cooperates with the staff. The bad patient is noisy, asks too many questions about his or her care, and is guilty of noncompliance with regard to medication and the chain of command. Many patients in nursing homes arrive with the hope of learning to be independent again, if only in a limited way. This hope is thwarted by the negativistic attitudes regarding patients who "make waves." A "wave maker" is one who will not sit passively by, waiting to go to the bathroom, to be changed, or to have pain medication. These *bad* patients often turn inward and become passive since they have learned that this independent behavior is frowned upon. They are victims of Seligman's "learned helplessness," which is also viewed negatively in institutions. (Seligman in Zarit, 1980, pp. 200-201) These people are not contributing to their treatment . . . a must for every good patient. What then is our frail elderly patient to do in this "double bind" situation where staff expectations conflict with staff instructions? The usual outcome is depression, more dependency, more ego loss leading to passive or "active" suicide. (Osgood, Brant & Lipman, 1988, pp. 69-78)   The accumulated losses, the existential crises that are commonplacecommonplace for our elderly, have always beset humankind. Since suicide seems to be a path that is often taken, despite religious and secular prohibition, the next chapter will explore suicide in its historical context.

NOTES

1. This behavior was prevalent in the senior center I directed, even though this particular population was younger and more socially active than other groups in Bucks County, PA.

III

An Historical Overview
of Suicide

Our beliefs about suicide and a physician's duties toward his or her patients rest on a foundation that took many thousands of years to accrue. Religious and political forces have shaped and reshaped various levels of this foundation, leaving it permeated with pockets of doubt and rare nuggets of wisdom. Knowing that humankind has continuously struggled to answer the same questions will help us to address modern dilemmas with regard to the appropriate use of technology, the preservation of the quality of life and the relief of suffering.

ANCIENT GREECE & ROME

During the classical period of Greece (5th century B.C.E.) physicians were itinerant, traveling from place to place to ply their skills, and held the status of craftsmen. Competing with each other, success was based on accurate diagnosis, and if possible, effective cure. In an essay entitled "The Acts," part of what is known as the "Hippocratic Collection," the physician in the role of healer was required to "do away with the sufferings of the sick, to lessen the violence of their diseases, and to refuse to treat those who are overwhelmed by their disease, realizing that in such cases medicine is powerless. (Humphrey & Wickett, 1986, p.4) The Greeks stripped suicide of much of its horror and superstition and elevated it as a subject worthy of rational discourse and consideration. Socrates argued that no one has a right to decide the manner and time of one's own death (Plato, *Phaedo* 62b-c) since human beings are the property of the gods. Variations of this argument, giving control over death to the gods, or to one deity alone, have become the most widespread justification for maintaining the idea that suicide is immoral. The argument that one has a duty to the human community, and in particular to the state was a common debate. Aristotle opposed suicide on the grounds that it treats the state unjustly. (EN 1138a 11-13) Obviously, this depends on what one understands the nature and function of the state to be. In a totalitarian regime, the state's goals are paramount, and overriding those of its citizens may even extend to the prohibition of suicide. In this instance, decisions of life and death rightfully belong to the state alone. (Moskop, et al, 1979, pp. 49-57)

In Rome, suicide was punishable only if it was irrational. Anyone who killed himself without cause was looked down upon because whoever does not spare himself would much less spare another. On the other hand, ending one's life because of terminal illness was considered good cause. (Humphrey, 1986, p.5) Josephus, the noted historian, was aware of the casual view of suicide held by Romans, especially those of higher status. So common was death by unnatural means, most usually suicide, the Roman historian Tacitus, when noting the death from natural causes of an aged pontiff, stated that this was a rare occurrence for a person of prominence (Annals 6.10) This particular pontiff died around 37 A.D., the year that Josephus was born. When Josephus speaks of Masada in his works he does not express admiration for the decision to commit mass suicide but attributes these feelings to the Roman soldiers. (Hankoff:1979, pp. 44-45)

JUDEAO-CHRISTIAN BELIEFS

In the study of suicide, it is important to examine the historical roots of the Judeao-Christian sanctions against taking one's own life. The general prohibition on bloodshed is reiterated time and again in the first five books of the Hebrew Bible (the Pentateuch) but no description of either a suicidal act or impulse is to be found there. (Hankoff, 1979, p. 4) Commandments commonly known as the Noachian precepts, rules for moral behavior after the "Deluge," are found in the book of Genesis. There *is* a prohibition against the spilling of man's blood. (Genesis 9:5) The formulation of the concept, which is reiterated many times in the Pentateuch, can be studied by looking at the ancient Near

East civilizations surrounding the Hebrews, and by researching suicides mentioned in the post-Pentateuchal books of the bible. Hankoff found six biblical references to suicide (self destructive behavior) and several examples of individuals who considered death as a solution to their despair. (pp. 5-7) All of the six suicides were plausible, with clear-cut precipitance or situations giving an understandable explanation for the self-destruction. All were males in the midst of rapidly moving situations, mortal danger or in a state of physical stress. All but one were prominent people whose positions of leadership were seriously damaged or threatened.

An interesting question that may shed light on the problem comes out of the idea of blood itself. Was the ancient prohibition on bloodshed a literal one, or was blood used as a metaphor for life? One might attempt to answer these by approaching the idea of personal responsibility outlined in the Hebrew Bible: Personal responsibility for one's life is indicated in those situations where, through negligence, one may expose oneself to death. The one who exposes him/herself to danger unnecessarily, "His blood shall be upon his own head." In Biblical references to execution, we find that in capital punishment, the *perpetrator* is responsible for the loss of his own life.

Crushing, hanging and burning to commit suicide are linked to the tenet of the avoidance of bloodshed. Except for those few who, in war killed themselves with their weapons, all are basically bloodless forms of suicide. The spilling of blood was dangerous to the community; this would be a breach in the covenant with God, and since ritual purity was extremely important (Leviticus) the horror of an unattended corpse in the wilderness could give rise to ritual or actual pollution. Human sacrifice, such as Jonah's multiple offers, are counteracted by miracles, and his suicidal ideation (which having a voluntary element was akin to more ancient practices) lead the researcher to believe that this practice was frowned upon; repentance and forgiveness are the theme of the book, not impulsive requests for death. We might conjecture that when human sacrifice was condemned by this society, self-sacrifice such as suicide also required condemnation. (Hankoff, 1979, pp. 18-19).

The aforementioned Josephus Flavius is one of the few writers of this era, according to Hankoff, who is relatively faithful to his sources. (Hankoff, 1979, pp. 34-38) His accounts of method, gender and philosophy allow us to look at the individual as well as trends in self-destructive behavior.

The suicide act in the first century A.D. was usually carried out by men rather than women, more often in groups than alone, and as a means to escape death that was imminent from another source. (Hankoff, 1979, p. 42) A variety of methods were used, many very painful, and the sword is most often noted as the tool of destruction. Hankoff suggests that open warfare induced a readiness for dying, and an impetuosity that enabled the defeated person to accept either suicide or death in battle. The combatant usually used his weapon on himself in defiance, despair or frustration. Josephus notes 24 fatal incidents in his writings: 16 are in battle or in settings of open hostility with death being a step away at the hands of an adversary. Therefore, death by suicide, for Josephus, is a natural extension of defeat in battle and the avoidance of its consequences which may be torture, sexual abuse, enslavement and public abuse of one's family or tribe. More often than not the execution of the captured soldier was the norm.

Of the 26 methods discussed by Josephus, the most common, as was stated, was the sword or knife. (12 out of 26 incidents recorded) The other methods were crushing, head-smashing, jumping, burning, drowning and hanging. Hankoff notes the striking omission of suicide by poison, and states that poisoning was a constant fear of the ancient ruler (hence the establishment of official "tasters") and that poisons were readily available. Drunkenness and wine abuse are not reported as being associated with attempted or completed suicides, in contrast to contemporary studies. (pp. 42-43)

With regard to gender issues, women were rarely central characters in history as Josephus perceived it. The only female suicide specifically mentioned is Cleopatra, and the only female reported as attempting suicide is the wife of someone named Pheroras (her name is never reported). Suicide of women along with men is suggested in the reporting of mass suicides, but all are nameless, and the historian gives the impression that men often destroyed their families and then committed suicide.

CHURCH LAW AND THE CATHOLIC WORLD

As early as the second and third centuries the Greek and Roman attitudes toward suicide was undermined by the influence of Christianity. Church law was profoundly affected. Anyone who took his own life was denied Christian burial. Civil legislation, reflecting divine law was influenced; not only were the victim's goods and property confiscated by civil authorities, the corpse received an ignominious burial on the highway, impaled by a stake. No exceptions were allowed, not even for those who had endured prolonged suffering due to an incurable, debilitating illness. Man owed all to God. Death was considered God's will and God's only. (Humphrey & Wickett, 1986, pp. 5-6)

Physicians could not be indifferent to open condemnation of suicide; such widespread disapproval affected their attitudes, especially toward patients who wanted to be put out of their misery. As had been proclaimed by the church, and the state, the taking of one's own life, under any circumstances, was prohibited. Every citizen was expected to abide by this . . . not least of all the physician.

By the 6th century, contractual agreements between a doctor and a patient were drawn up, often in writing . . . and during this time the relationship between the medical and lay communities had also become more structured. By the 12th century groups of practitioners had banded together into worker associations. More tightly controlled standards of training, education and performance were the result, and in 1140, state examinations were held in Sicily for those who wanted to practice medicine. (Veatch, 1981, pp. 128-30) Over the next two hundred years this kind of legislation evolved in other countries. Physicians' guilds became established medical schools and their recognition as the arbiter of standards was exchanged for the public's right to play a role in setting the terms of professional practice.

In 533 the council of Orleans declared that funeral rites would be denied to any one who had killed himself while accused of a crime, formerly approved of by the early philosophers as a method of saving the state the trouble and preserving the dignity (Roman 'dignitas') of those in intolerable political circumstances. Three decades later, the Council of Braga proscribed funeral rites to *all* suicides, regardless of social position, method or circumstances. This would have included most of those who martyred themselves for the church. (Farberow, 1975, pp. 6-7) Several ethicists and historians have used this fine point to state that suicide prohibitions at this juncture were mainly to stop the inordinate flood of ill-considered martyrdom that may have been embarrassing to the church. (Portwood, 1978, pp. 11-14)

In 693, the Council of Toledo announced that anyone who attempted suicide would be excommunicated. It was here, at this time of new medical knowledge from non-Christian societies, that the contract between the physician and the patient started to unravel, and the newly professional healer was bound to the Christian guild and state. (Humphrey, 1986)

Culminating in the 13th century with St. Thomas Aquinas' *Summa Theologica,* suicide violated the 6th commandment, it was the most dangerous of sins because it left no time for repentance. It was against the law of nature; the divine plan for creation is found in the laws of nature and among these laws is a tendency of everything to love and preserve itself. (ST 2a2ae 64,5). It was a sin against society since man belongs to his community and it was a sin against the diety because life was a gift and subject only to God's powers. It was the most mortal of Christian sins. (Moskop, 1979)

Paradoxically, many village churches in England had what was termed "the Holy Maul" to help elderly sufferers into the next world. Akin to stunning an ox with a club, the maul was used secretly, but extensively in the 14th and 15th century. Ruth Nichols, in her book, *The Burning of the Rose*, states that "The Holy Maul is a hammer that hangs behind certain church doors and with the priest's blessing, ends old lives when Nature has proven cruel." (1990: p. 176) One must always keep in mind the anthropological tenet that ideal behavior and real behavior within a society may be farther apart than is imagined; even within a highly structured organization such as the church.

A SHIFT IN ATTITUDE

During the Renaissance and Reformation that followed, a shift in the attitude toward suicide began to emerge. There was more of an emphasis on the individual in society. Religious values began to change from absolutism and strict obedience to the church, to personal inquiry and personal responsibility. Orthodox Protestantism gave man the right to question, to doubt and to challenge that which had formerly been taken for granted. Along with these new theological freedoms, however, came a sense of isolation and self-consciousness. Calvanism, appearing at the same time, had an opposite approach; God was exalted and inaccessible in His superiority. This tended to minimize and humble the individual, the question of the value of the human soul was raised. Italy experienced a renewal of learning this brought to light classical ideas about human nature, diminishing the horror of well reasoned suicide. (Farberow, 1975, p. 8) Sir Thomas More, writing about suicide and euthanasia in his Utopia (1516), shows a remarkably reasonable attitude toward the subject (Turner, 1981, p. 102), as did Montaigne in humanistic writings of the period. Using Cato the Stoic as his model, tempered by moderate Christianity, he wrote, "Death is a most assured haven, never to be feared, and often to be sought." "All comes to one period, whether man make an end to himself, or whether he endure it." (Fedden, 1938, p. 162)

As the Renaissance spread, individuals began to find life more and more intolerable because of a new awareness of poverty and lack of a future. There was a preoccupation with death, melancholy and an awareness psychological complexity. In Shakespeare's productions, we find Hamlet contemplating suicide, as well as Prospero and Lear. In Shakespeare's eight tragedies, there are no less than 14 suicides. Sir Richard Burton (1621), in his *Anatomy of Melancholy*, broke with church dogma and questioned the tenet of eternal damnation of suicide. John Donne wrote the first defense of suicide in English in 1644. *Biathanatos* dealt with the practical side of the act, and stated openly that each man must be judged individually, since circumstances alter each case of suicide. The educated groups readily tolerated suicide at this time, but among the lower classes, the Church was staunchly opposed to suicide. This created reactionary secular legislation in

England that called suicide not only murder, but high treason and heresy. (Farberow, 1975, pp. 8-9)

Hume's essay *On Suicide* (1783), argues that individual humans are of such little account in the grand scheme of the universe that their actions are incapable of upsetting the Divine order. Further, it is postulated, if one could disturb Divine providence by committing suicide, then any attempt to protect one's life from natural dangers would disturb it as well. (Moskop, 1979) Suicide was not a crime against God because He gave man the power to act and therefore death at one's own hand was as much under God's control as if it had proceeded from any other source. Hume wrote that suicide was not a breach against society, since in the act, there is no harm, only a cessation of the ability to do good. He also stated that suicide cannot be a crime against self because he felt that not many ever threw away a life that was still worth keeping. (Evans & Farberow, 1988, p. xix) At the same time, new arguments appeared that made a distinction between morality and emotional illness. This argument was extended to postulate that all suicides were mentally ill in some degree and paved the way for the church to skirt it's own laws against suicide, by issuing the verdict of "suicide while of unsound mind." (1988, p. xix)

MORE RECENT ATTITUDE CHANGES

During the 19th century, the strongest bulwarks against suicide, religious tenets and social stigma, began to lose effectiveness. Capitalism created a new economic interdependence, but fostered social isolation adding to the difficulties of those who were most at risk for suicide. Scientific writing began to appear, medical theories were postulated, social science began to discover commonalties and patterns (Durkheim, 1897), and the idea of assisted suicide (voluntary euthanasia) was again discussed by the medical community. Still bound by laws promulgated by the dictates of church and state, even though in many instances illegally so (ie: religious views of the value of suffering), a few outspoken physicians began to chafe at restrictions that seemed inhumane. One such physician, in 1873, wrote an article entitled, "The New Cure of the Incurables." It was a strong plea for the legalization of voluntary euthanasia. "Need I not add," he wrote, "that, if a doctor, even at an agonized patient's entreaty, takes a course likely to hasten death, he is doing that for which, under the present law, he might be severely taken to task; nay, that he is hovering on the brink of manslaughter, if not of something worse?" (Tollemache, 1873)

At the First Euthanasia Conference, Nov. 23, 1968, Rev. Robert Reeves, Jr. on discussing the Right to Die Laws stated,

> . . . they do not directly address the slowly progressive, chronic, totally incapacitating medical diseases of the heart, kidneys, lungs, brain, and liver—the vital organs. Moreover, since these laws are only applicable in the terminal two weeks of your life, they are of no help in avoiding months or years in a convalescent hospital. (in Baer, 1978, p. 108)

TODAY

At time of this writing, suicide is still a crime in several American states. A few states, such as California, have presented legislative bills to legalize some forms of medical euthanasia. Obviously, inextricably bound domains such as religion and law, giving direction to medical training and practice cannot begin to address the needs of individuals unless physicians and their patients speak to those who influence policy. This must be done before need, since it is too easy to make a case for "mental instability" while a patient is experiencing emotional or physical pain.

"The cry, save me doctors, has turned to save me from machines, doctor," according to Humphrey and Wickett. The report that "mercy killings" rose ten times in the 1980's compared to any five-year period since 1920, while murder-suicide, double suicides, and assisted suicides involving the terminally ill increased forty times as desperate elderly people felt obliged to the take the law and fate into their own hands. (Humphrey & Wickett, 1986, p. xi) Medicine caters to the biological man, often abandoning the psychological and social one. Pneumonia, formerly the 'old man's friend" is treated with antibiotics. The patient lingers--often in pain. Afraid of litigation, the medical team persists.

The medical team is made up of individuals. The primary care physician is the liaison, in many cases, between the institution and the patient, and if necessary, the patient's family. It is this physician who is closest to the patient, and it is this physician whose attitude toward death will probably determine the course of treatment; to refer the patient elsewhere, or to help with pain control and emotional support . . . or even supply the means for a dignified death.

The next chapter elicits the concerns and practices of a small sample of physicians in a preliminary attempt to understand the attitudes that give rise to today's medical practices.

IV

The Study of Physicians' Attitudes Toward Elder Suicide

AN INTRODUCTION

The phenomenon of elder suicide is reaching problematic proportions in the United States. Most family physicians, much like the physicians in this study, have little or no training in geriatric medicine and may be unfamiliar with the dynamics that underlie elder suicide. This study was designed to question the belief systems of those general practitioners and determine if those attitudes lead to a difference in treatment when suicide is suspected.

While much has been written regarding the reasons for this trend, little non-anecdotal material has been published regarding the attitude of those who are charged with the care and maintenance of the physical well being of those who are considered elderly. According to the American Association of Suicidology, the Suicide Information Center in Calgary, Alberta and various medical and sociological library collections, no studies of these physicians' attitudes regarding elder suicide exist at this time. Therefore, the following research should be viewed as a pilot study.

METHODOLOGY

The Respondents

This investigation of attitudes and behaviors was accomplished by personal interviews with twenty white, male, Bucks County, Pennsylvania general practitioners. Thirty physicians were chosen, at random, from the Bucks County, PA telephone directory after the elimination of female and non-occidental names. They were then contacted by letter (see Appendix A), with a follow up phone call if no response was forthcoming. Three physicians had their secretaries call for appointments within two weeks of receiving the letter; twenty-seven required one or two phone calls to schedule appointments. Five physicians declined to participate due to what was characterized as "over-busy schedules;" one family doctor was eliminated since he was no longer practicing in the area, and one physician could not be included due to a different practice specialty than listed. Black physicians are not widely represented in Bucks County and were not found in the chosen sample. If they had been, plans were in place to interview the black physician, rather than ask about the race of the respondent when making the appointment, and use their comments in a later study or a "reflection piece" to highlight our sample's particular beliefs.

It was decided that the inclusion of female physicians would confound the study since their attitudes may be more reflective of society's traditional nurturant role ascription than their role as a physician. Traditional male roles tend to have less hands-on nurturant structures; the emphasis has been on financial nurturance. Sociological studies indicate that males define themselves, to a large extent, by their work role. (Goffman, 1963, p. 17) Therefore, they would present a less confused belief configuration for the assessment of physicians' attitudes.

Doctors of Osteopathic Medicine (D.O.) and Doctors of Allopathic Medicine (M.D.) are equally represented in Lower Bucks County, and care was taken to show this distribution.

The Interview

The interviews were structured as to content (ie: attitudes toward suicide in general, mental health referrals for the elderly, medications, etc). The physician was not told that the attitudes and behaviors related to the suicide of elderly patients was the focus of this inquiry. They were, however, apprised of my interest in physician's attitudes toward suicide and its etiology in the introductory letter. (Appendix A). Questions dealing with passive and active euthanasia and life support were included, since these issues are related to assisted suicide. These questions also served as controls, since a physician would be unlikely to be against suicide and for euthanasia.

Those interviewed were audio-taped by the principle researcher, who also had a check-list of topics to be covered. The interviews, at times, became unstructured so as to give the physician a chance for further reflection. 30 request letters were sent, and 20 interviews were scheduled and completed. 57% of the D.O.'s agreed to the interview; 67% of the M.D.'s agreed to meet with the researcher. All of the physicians were in family or general practice. The average length of interview was twenty-five minutes.

The categories of questions for the structured part of the interviews was culled from the material the researcher had already collected as a question pool for a possible Likert Scaling of this same material. This pool material was accumulated by questionnaires distributed to social workers at a Bucks County assistance office and to the general population (see Appendix B for pool material).

According to D. Mueller *(Measuring Social Attitudes,* 1986, pp. 88-89), interview data are considered valid if the same conclusions regarding elder suicide result from two separate interviews on the same subject. As this was extremely difficult to accomplish given the limited time that most general practitioners have been willing or able to devote to non-patients, the question of reliability was dealt with using Mueller's suggestions for correcting inconsistency of response on the part of the respondent, mistakes or inconsistencies in recording by the interviewer, and arbitrariness or bias in interpretation by the analyst of the data. The suggested mechanisms used for controlling these sources of unreliability were the editing of the questions for clarity, the repetition of certain questions in slightly different wording at different places in the interview, taping of each interview along with note-taking, and having a second and independent researcher analyze the recorded data. (see Appendix C for actual questions used) A fellow-intern at the Tulsa Psychiatric Center was recruited to listen to the tapes and their attendant forms; interrater reliability was shown to be 98%.

After the interviews were completed and tapes checked for accuracy, the responses were noted in table form and converted to percentages.

THE RESULTANT DATA COLLECTED
FOR EACH PARAMETER

Years in Practice

The most frequent score, the mode = 4 years in practice. The median = 16.5 years in practice. This median was used as a distinction (for brevity) regarding more or less years in practice. For example, those with more than 16.5 years were grouped together, as well as those below 16.5 in order to simplify reporting and to ascertain if years in practice was an important *independent* variable. Eleven physicians were located above the median in practice years (< 16.5, designated group 1); nine physicians were located below the median in practice years (> 16.5, designated group 2).

Percentage of Geriatric Patients

The most frequent percentage of geriatric population reported in the physicians' practice was 20%. The median percentage of geriatric patients was 23.5%. 67% of Group 2 had the most geriatric patients (average population percent-age, 46.7), while 91% of Group 1 had the lowest percentage of geriatric patients (average population percentage 17.3).

ANALYSIS OF GROUP 1

Group 1 was comprised of eleven physicians with 2 to 15 years in general practice. Two of these physicians had the majority of the elderly patients reported by the group.

    Six members of this group stated that they thought the same about suicide for any age group (whether negative or positive) and would treat those suspected of suicidal intent the same, regardless of age. Five physicians stated that they thought more positively about suicide for the elderly and noted that they would treat suicidal patients according to age (ie: hospitalization, family involvement, medication, counseling, etc.). (It appears that physicians in our study having less than 16.5 in practice are fairly evenly divided on the above issues.) The physicians who thought the same about suicide regardless of age also stated that mental illness was present if the elderly were well, but still wanted to commit suicide. Eight of eleven members of Group 1 approved of suicide for the terminally ill. With regard to having more approval toward elder suicide, five members disapproved of suicide for any aged person, and four were more approving toward elder suicide than for younger individuals. Only two physicians in this group approved of suicide for the terminally ill of any age. As there is a discrepancy between initial approval for suicide of the terminally ill and the rate of disapproval when members of this group were asked to qualify their statements (see #4 and #5 of study results with regard to attitude), one wondered if there was a pattern developing to show the likelihood of different answers for generic questions, and specifics subsumed within the topic. When the "blanket" question was posited whether anyone had the right to take their own life, seven of eleven stated "yes." This highlights the deep conflict regarding suicide among many professionals. Since we all have experienced early socialization by cultural values and family mores, one cannot separate the physician from the "man."

In the area of assisted suicide, or "voluntary euthanasia" as some writers are labeling the act, seven members of Group 1 stated that it may be acceptable for family members to assist the patient to die. Only one of the physicians approving of family help stated that physicians should be able to assist.

Six members of Group 1 stated that they thought the same about active or passive suicide (withdrawal of medication, life supports, etc.), while four found that passive suicide was more acceptable to them. (Only one physician stated that an active attempt was preferable, due to the very long time a person may linger after supports have ceased.)

Life support for the elderly was overwhelmingly approved by all members of the group, with most adding a qualifier dependent on circumstances: the patient's wishes, and condition of the patient. The variable of age was not considered important by this group.

Six physicians reported having a patient commit suicide, and they were evenly matched with regard to method (three by violent means, three by passive means). No patients over 65 were reported as having committed suicide. Eight members reported that they had directly asked patients if they were contemplating suicide. Eight also stated that they were comfortable in their skills in assessing suicide risk. It is important to note that the reasons they gave for elder suicide tended to be symptoms such as depression brought on by loss of spouse, etc., rather than the actual cues such as buying weapons, stockpiling pills, or giving away possessions. (Secouler & Tronetti: 1986)

Only one physician in the group attended a formal geriatric medicine class, but suicide was not discussed. Two respondents stated that they had discussed suicide in pharmacy school and only with regard to overdosage of medication.

When queried as to the group most at risk for suicide, six members stated "the elderly;" nine were aware of the high rate of elder suicide, with the majority of this group citing reading material as the source of this awareness.

ANALYSIS OF GROUP 2

Group 2 is comprised of nine physicians with 19 to 39 years in general practice. Four of the practitioners had 67% of the reported geriatric patients—a more even distribution than found in Group 1.

Seven respondents reported feeling the same (negative or positive) about suicide, regardless of age. Two of the nine members stated that they thought more positively about the suicide of the elderly. Five members of Group 2 stated that they would treat suicidal patients the same, regardless of age, while four thought that differing modalities might be in order. Six of the respondents thought that mental illness is present with suicidal ideation in the well elderly, and only a small cadre (three of nine members), approved of suicide for the terminally ill. When asked if they would be more accepting of a older person's suicide as compared to a younger person (to elicit attitudinal changes during the interview and to qualify their acceptance or non-acceptance), five physicians stated that they did not approve of suicide for any age group. Two members of Group 2 stated that they approved regardless of age, and one physician thought differently about age groups and was more approving of elder suicide. When faced with the question, "Does anyone have the right to take his/her life," four members stated that the right exists, and an equal number stated that it did not, and one member of was not sure. There appears to be less attitudinal change with regard to moving from the general to the specific with this group, which may indicate a more concrete position on suicide. Whether this is based on experience, early medical training or a combination of factors is unknown; the physicians themselves stated that personal morality rather than the Hippocratic Oath was the underlying factor.

Seven members of Group 2 stated that it was not acceptable for family members to help someone to commit suicide--and again, these seven stated that it should not be made legal for physicians to assist with "voluntary euthanasia" or assisted suicide. Passive suicide, the withdrawal of medication and life support, was more acceptable to the seven respondents than an active attempt.

Life support for the elderly was overwhelming approved by Group 2 with the following qualifications: three stated that it should be on a limited basis; five based it on unspecified circumstances that did not include age as a factor.

Eight members of Group 2 had patients who committed suicide; three reported non-violent (overdoses) methods, and five reported violent means such as hanging, gun use and obvious vehicular suicide (autocide). Group 2 reports that two patients who were 65+ and one 55+ were included in the suicide survey. Only one physician had not knowingly experienced the loss of a patient to suicide.

All of the physicians in Group 2 had asked patients "point-blank" if they were contemplating suicide. Two stated that the elderly were most at risk for suicide; seven reported awareness of a high rate. Of the seven physicians reporting awareness, five stated that reading was the source of this knowledge; two reported that experience in general practice fostered their insight.

Group 2 was evenly divided in their comfort or discomfort in skills assessing suicide risk. Only one member had attended a formal geriatric medicine class, and suicide was not mentioned. One respondent attended a continuing medical education (C.M.E.) seminar on aging, and suicide *was* on the agenda.

Table 2: Comparison of Groups 1 & 2

Years in Practice	*1-15*	*19-39*	*Differ.*
More positive about elder suicide	*.45*	*.22*	*.23**
Control statement re: elder suicide	*.36*	*.11*	.25*
Tx according to age	.46	.44	.02
Mental illness present	.55	.67	.12
Approve of suicide for term. ill	.73	.33	.40*
OK for family help in suicide	.64	.22	.42*
It should be legal for Doc to help	.36	.22	.14
More approval passive euthanasia	.36	.78	.42*
There is a right to die	.64	.44	.20*
Life support for elderly OK	1.00	1.00	.00
Experienced suicide in practice	.54	.89	.35*
Knowledge that elders most at risk	.55	.44	.11
Aware of high risk for elders	.82	.78	.04
Reading material was knowledge source	.45	.55	.10
Have asked point-blank about plans	.73	1.00	.27*
Comfortable about suicide knowledge	.73	.11	.62*
Geriatrics class attendance	.09	.11	.02

* denotes more than 20% differential

CONCLUSIONS

The figures indicate that within this population, physicians with less years (16.5) in practice were more approving of elder suicide specifically, and more approving of suicide for the terminally ill, in general. They were more likely than physicians with 19+ years in practice to approve of relatives helping the patient to die, and were slightly more positive about a physician legally helping with voluntary euthanasia. The less experienced group was more knowledgeable about the high risk of elder suicide, although each group was equal in that only one member attended a formal geriatrics medicine class in school. A strong positive response toward patient autonomy with regard to the right to die was shown, as compared to a low positive response from Group 2.

Those with more years in practice (19-39) tended to feel better than their younger counterparts on the issue of passive suicide versus an active attempt. They were more likely to ask a patient point-blank if suicide was an issue, but felt less comfortable with their assessment skills with regard to suicide than Group 1.

Both groups had many members who would take age into consideration with regard to treatment; the main difference between the two groups was the inclusion of family notification for younger potential suicides. Medication, referral for in-patient psychological help and out-patient psychiatry were all discussed depending on the physician's view of immediate need. All physicians used the physical symptoms of depression as a cue to potential suicide, as well as some well known psycho-social aspects such as recent bereavement. None, however, mentioned cues such as the buying of a weapon, stockpiling pills, having a timetable, or changing of wills. "Point-blank" questions to patients regarding suicide usually entailed asking if the patient was considering committing suicide. Follow-up questions regarding means did not occur unless the patient stated that he or she was contemplating taking this step, but no physician reported having a patient tell them that a suicide was being planned. Therefore, one must assume that in this population of physicians, there may be a breakdown in communication between parties, or the right questions were not asked, since there were suicides reported by the respondents.

EXCERPTS FROM THE TAPED INTERVIEWS

Group #1 Physician #7—4 years in Practice (50% geriatric)

Q: How do you feel about elderly suicide, as compared to other age groups?

A: Given some of the circumstances that some of these people are laboring under . . . I don't know if it's so totally off the wall. It's a shame. Ironically, you do everything you can to keep somebody alive in the hospital who is dying of some terminal disease. What are you supposed to do? Your mate dies . . . you are 80 years old . . .what are you supposed to do, go out an find another woman and change the last seven years of your life? There is less horror in elder suicide for me, given some of the circumstances. Depending, also, on the manner in which its done.

Q: How would you treat an elderly suspected suicide as compared to another age group?

A: I wouldn't treat them differently. If I think somebody is on the verge of doing something . . . I would have them come back the next day, or refer them to someone. Is there family to talk to . . . is there someone else that I want to get involved? I take that into consideration. Some need an audience, but are not really going to do it. I have to go on gut feelings. Some need a psychiatric referral with hospitalization.

Q: If an elderly person was physically well, but still wanted to commit suicide, how would you view this?

A: I don't see why someone who is depressed is necessarily mentally ill . . . or physically ill. There could be a change in life circumstances. Until clarified, however . . . I still consider it possible mental illness.

Q: Would you approve of suicide for a terminally ill person?

A: Sure. Any age. If you have established that the patient is terminally ill, and if the patient is sure. I'm kind of surpised that it doesn't happen more often.

Q: How do you feel about family members helping someone to commit suicide?

A: If you have a terminally ill person, I suppose that would be within reason. You have be sure that you wouldn't be walking around with that guilt for the rest of your life . . . or in jail.

Q: Should it be legal for a physician to help someone die if that is their wish?

A: Terminally ill . . . yes. There's a fundamental conflict here with a physician treating the whole person . . . and what if a person were not terminally ill, but would be better off dead . . . good question. A lot of these old people say, "Give me the pill . . . so that if I don't want it (the suffering) any longer, I don't have to take it. I don't want to sit and suffer like my friend Max did," or whatever. I would like to be able to tell someone who is terminally ill what to take, or to legally provide something that would work for them. If someone has a condition that they are in pain, day in and day out . . . and the pain is terminal, not the condition . . . and they are living on morphine. To me this is a terminal disease, because it will finally cause their death by breaking them down physically, immunologically, whatever. Actually, a more active attempt, rather than withdrawal of medication or nutrition would be better for the patient. They would be less uncomfortable. Starvation, dehydration takes a long time.

Q: Does anyone have the right to take their own life?

A: Yes. Just as I stated before.

Physician #4—13 years in Practice. (10% geriatric population)

Q: How do you feel about elderly suicide, as compared to other age groups?

A: I think that people in the older age group who commit suicide are doing it as a relief or a solution to frustration and problems. I usually feel . . . not better, but relieved more often, because they were suffering from cancer . . . or something else. In other words, there was more of a reason for them to commit suicide than for the others to commit suicide. It was a better solution at that age than at a younger age.

Q: How would you treat an elderly suspected suicide as compared to another age group?

A: Number one, I would probably take it more seriously, but I might not be nearly as aggressive as I would be with a younger person. I would treat them with anti-depressants and refer them to a psychiatrist or a psychologist. I think with the younger ones I would continue to insist that they get psychological help and would not treat them further until they obtained help. The older ones, I would make sure they got help eventually, but I wouldn't keep calling them every five minutes to make sure they got help. I think in both cases I would contact family members, or people that were close to make sure that they (the patient) were also under close supervision so that they would do what I wanted them to. I wouldn't be as quick with the older group to insist on certain kinds of help. I think that they know what they are doing, they thought these things out more, and they are more aware of reasons for what they are doing. They're more responsible. I kind of think that when they get that age, they don't need someone nagging at them. They know what to do. They may not want to do it, but they know what to do.

Q: If an elderly person was physically well, but still wanted to commit suicide, how would you view this?

A: I don't consider them to be physically well if they are suicidal. There is something unwell in the physical aspect as well as the mental aspect. If there is a chemical imbalance, if they are depressed, they are physically not well. That has to be addressed.

Q: Would you approve of suicide for a terminally ill person?

A: I definitely believe that if they are suffering they should be allowed . . . at whatever age . . . if they are terminal, to end their suffering. Especially if it is euthanasia. By that, I mean passive . . . pulling the plug on technology. I definitely feel better about that than using a gun. I suppose pills might be OK in certain circumstances. If there is no machine to disconnect in order to end suffering.

Q: How do you feel about family members helping someone to commit suicide?

A: That occurred . . . a physician I know helped his mother. I don't disapprove of what he did for his mother. He got arrested, and I don't agree with the courts. A time will come when it will be legal. It's the circumstance rather than the age . . . although the age is a strong consideration.

Q: Should it be legal for a physician to help someone die if that is their wish?

A: If that's their wish, sure. And if the circumstances are of the sort if there is hopelessness and no alternative solution . . . that would be appropriate.

Q: Does anyone have the right to take their own life?

A: I believe that a person should have control of their life and if they are able to make a clear decision . . . if they are competent to make a decision from the legal standpoint. If they have that capacity, I believe that they should be able to do whatever they want.

Group #2 Physician #11—28 years in practice (60% Geriatric population)

Q: How do you feel about elderly suicide, as compared to other age groups?

A: Well, it's a little disturbing. There probably should be more support for those people. I'm equally disturbed by suicide in any age group.

Q: How would you treat an elderly suspected suicide as compared to another age group?

A: I'd say the same. It depends on the severity. Most of the depressions we see are mild. You just give them a little support. But anybody who appears to be severely depressed, I'd probably have a psychiatric referral.

Q: If an elderly person was physically well, but still wanted to commit suicide, how would you view this?

A: I would be a little alarmed about it. I would be very cautious about how I would handle it. Mental illness is probably present.

Q: Would you approve of suicide for a terminally ill person?

A: No. It doesn't matter what age they are. Not even if it is only the withdrawal of medication . . . passive.

Q: How do you feel about family members helping someone to commit suicide?

A: No. Definitely not.

Q: Should it be legal for a physician to help someone die if that is their wish?

A: I don't agree with that.

Q: Does anyone have the right to take their own life?

A: No.

Physician #13—35 years in Practice (80% Geriatric population)

Q: How do you feel about elderly suicide, as compared to other age groups?

A: Well it is always a tragedy when people feel that type of abandonment . . . or emotional despair. I would be less shocked, or have less of a consternation about an older individual committing suicide, or making a suicide attempt. In the younger individual, you can see that they are bypassing a lot of potential that, for some reason, they are not aware of. With the older individual you can see that they are reaching a time of life where this potential has been satisfied or frustrated, and they are not going to make any recovery.

Q: How would you treat an elderly suspected suicide as compared to another age group?

A: First I would allow them to ventilate what they have on their mind. I would not give any opinions, except in the sense of acknowledging unfavorable situations . . . older patients. The younger individual, you look for different things altogether. The younger individual, I would rather refer for a psychiatric evaluation. They are more apt to act more precipitously than the older individual. The older individual probably has had thoughts of any significance about suicide for a longer time, and they are more apt to be mulling over the thing, and there is less likely to be a definite mention.

Q: If an elderly person was physically well, but still wanted to commit suicide, how would you view this?

A: Well, I would look to see if there is a depression, or certain physical conditions that were not recognized. If all of these things were ruled out . . . I still cannot agree that this is a rational thing to do. Suicide. This is a selfish impulse or decision. And you are really not thinking about what family there is, or who might be affected.

Q: Would you approve of suicide for a terminally ill person?

A: I don't think that I could agree to active suicide. I cannot be quite sure of my reactions to passive suicide . . . I might agree with an evaluation of the circumstances to withhold certain treatments. There's an aspect to this that goes beyond the individual. Suicide has social significance. If it is allowed in certain conditions, that are spelled out in bureaucratic black-and-white terms, then that's the only solution necessary. For example, in 1900 there was no cure for TB, or for many things . . . like syphilis. If the solution at that time was to take your leave, there would be no need for going any further. Say with cancer . . . no need for further research to cure the problem. You've got the solution. In battle conditions there are horrible wounds and many men beg for death. If they got the individual back to the MASH unit they might be saved and have a decent life . . . a lot of men would have died if they had been given the coup de grace on the battle field. The doctor that's dealing with elderly patients cannot fall into the trap of being fatalistic. You can't just say, "He's got nothing to live for." That's the personal point of view and it may or may not be proper for that person. Suicide probably doesn't represent a desire to end a life . . . but a desire to get the hell out of a bad situation. If they could get out of the situation without suicide, they are not going to commit suicide. There again, acknowledging the need to solve the problem . . . and not the need for suicide as a solution. That's true of many problems. Probably most doctors would say that there are not many people who want to die. They are looking for escape from unpleasant situations, really. Is there a fear of death, or a fear of suffering? Which is the big thing? I don't know.

Q: How do you feel about family members helping someone to commit suicide?

A: I think that would be a mistake. Most thinking of suicide is emotionally tinged, which is not wholly rational. No question about that there would be some people who would be enthusiastic to help overburdensome parents their "quietus make."

Q: Should it be legal for a physician to help someone die if that is their wish?

A: Here again, I think it is too generalized. I do not think it is legitimate to assist in active suicide. Now I can, given the certain circumstances, with not one individual, not one physician, making the decision, understand what is already done now . . . to withdraw unnecessary treatment. And that's a big factor. Withdrawing of nourishment is not the same as withholding medication . . . or technology. I believe in administering comfort.

Q: Does anyone have the right to take their own life?

A: I think everybody has the right to have the opinion that they are ready to take off . . . that they are ready to die, but I would be reluctant to give them the right to actually follow through. (This particular respondant was the oldest physician. He was in his mid-seventies at the time of the interview and had the most years in practice.)

SUBJECTIVE IMPRESSIONS AND COMMENTS ABOUT THE STUDY

During the interviews, it seemed to me that the younger physicians were actively struggling with paternalism; can one strip a patient of his or her rights with regard to preserving life, and for what purpose? The fact that they were younger leads me to presume that the majority still have living parents, and possibly grandparents, and their presence would increase reticence on the part of the grown "child" to usurp parental prerogatives. Future studies should include questions regarding the configuration of the physician's family if order to see if this conflict was a possible factor in attitude formation at this level.

The older physician's attitudes seem to reflect more of a relationship with the patient that is affected by being part of the same or close cohort. It may be more difficult for our older physician to distance himself, or become detached psychologically, from patients in his own age range. Identification with the older patient may create a barrier to accepting personal autonomy with regard to suicide. It if is not something they would contemplate in the same circumstances, it becomes harder to envision anyone else wanting to kill themselves. Death constitutes a major defeat for many physicians; how much harder would it be to accept death that was welcomed or planned for? Future studies should include personal questions about their own wishes in case of terminal illness, and also questions regarding the deaths of their contemporaries. As their own ages tend to decrease the number of antecedents still living, it would be fruitful to ask about family configurations, caregiving situations, etc.

It was not surprising to me that most of the physicians believed that mental illness was present when a patient wanted to commit suicide. The medical model of aging reinforces the idea of decay, decline and pathology. One is apt to consider the aging patient who is alert, active and vitally interested in the world as an anomaly, since wellness is not promoted nor encouraged by most of our insurance systems and is not a priority in medical schools with so little time to teach the pathology related to aging. "What do you expect, He's old," is still parroted by those who have not transcended the medical model.

The one physician who actually knew of a case where a clinician helped a parent (not a patient) to die was clearly distressed by the legal implications. He did not elaborate on the issue, even though he was encouraged to continue. His voice became extremely low, even though there was no apparent danger in this discussion of events. There seemed to be an unspoken agreement with the action taken, and it was this agreement that affected him as a physician. Most of the physicians gave the impression, but did not expressly admit, that they knew of clinicians who had helped patients to die. Facial expressions and shoulder shrugging during the interview seemed to be conveying what they were not verbally expressing.

Time was an important factor for most of the individuals involved in the study. The phones rang constantly in the consulting rooms, and the interviews were interrupted numerous times. The interviews lasted on the average of twenty-five minutes; a great deal of time for a busy office schedule. When the appointments were made, I advised the secretaries (my allies in the quest for appointments) that I would get there before hours, after hours ... and would even bring lunch if it facilitated my acceptance. However, most of the physicians gave me time during their afternoon sessions ... and this was the most distracting time of the day for them. Only one interview was scheduled at the local hospital. As a "thank you" for completed interviews, I presented each clinician with a copy of my recent article on elder suicide. (Secouler & Tronetti: 1989)

The seeming superficiality of the answers, I believe, came not from the reluctance to talk, but from the physical site of the interview, the interview format and the choice of questions. It would be hard to schedule physicians at home, therefore a possible choice might be a presentation on the subject as an in-service at a local institution with private questionnaires given as part of the program. Another choice might be sponsorship by a medical school or association at a medical convention of some sort, with a room set aside for interviews. As socializing is a big part of medical conventions, it would have to be done with continuing medical education credits (C.M.E.'s) as an offering.

The interview format was not a bad choice, but it was limited by the constraints of my personal paradigm and my data pool. One wonders what information might have been offered if the structure of the research design was even more qualitative.

The next step in this study of attitudes would be to include females and non-white physicians, change the format to include personal information, encourage communication by changing the setting (if possible), and focus less on the number of physicians giving the same answers and more on why the answers were given.

V

A Review of Recent Writings
Regarding Suicide

In light of our physicians' reported beliefs about elder suicide, and individual autonomy in terminal situations, we must review some of the writings that may have influenced this population. More than half of this population of physicians stated that their knowledge source was from reading material. It is important to note that our front-line physicians are not the academics who write for medical journals or chair ethics committees, and their attitudes may not reflect what is being postulated by others. (Overall, the physicians who were in practice for less than 15 years, and tended to be younger, were more positive about elder suicide, family assistance in helping someone to die, and significantly more positive about suicide for the terminally ill. Older physicians, with 19-39 years in practice were more approving of passive euthanasia, and tended to be against any active attempt to end a patient's life even if he/she suffered from a terminal illness.)

THE ETHICISTS

Moskop and Englehardt in their chapter "The Ethics of Suicide: A Secular View" (in Hankoff, 1979:49-57), discuss suicide through various moral paradigms; ie: in terms of the consequences involved in any particular choice based on a culture's view of what is due to a deity, to others, and what is due to oneself. They have placed the burden of proof upon those who, for whatever reason, hold that suicide is immoral.

The time-honored question of whether, should there be a God, we would owe a duty not to take our own lives is put forth, and the attitude of Socrates is reviewed. Socrates argued that no one has a right to decide the manner and time of one's own death (in Plato, *Phaedo* 62b-c) since human beings are the property of the gods. Variations of this argument, giving control over death to the gods, or to one deity alone, have become, according to the authors, the most widespread justification for maintaining the idea that suicide is immoral. Thomas Aquinas'(1225?-45) argument that the divine plan for creation is found in the laws of nature is mentioned; among these laws is a tendency of everything to love and preserve itself. (ST 2a2ae 64, 5) Moskop and Englehardt counter this with Hume's essay *On Suicide*, where the empiricist argues that individual humans are of such little account in the grand scheme of the universe that their actions are incapable of upsetting the Divine order. It is further postulated that if one could disturb Divine providence by committing suicide, then any attempt to protect one's life from natural dangers would disturb it as well. A reply to Hume might point out that God's omniscience implies that there is a concern for the life of each individual person, and human beings are not completely at the mercy of natural phenomena; rather there is a special charge to preserve and protect, and not to destroy the divine gift of life. The authors feel that this would appear to be a difficult point to make since the universe appears to be indifferent to the miseries of humans, and that human interference and intervention prevent a great deal of suffering. In short, without belief in an explicit divine proscription to taking one's own life, there would be little to support the theory that God opposes suicide. All of these arguments share a common limitation. They are dependent on a particular belief about God's will regarding the preservation of human life and indirectly on a set of religious beliefs about the existence and nature of God and His relationship with mankind. The authors postulate that an argument for a particular moral stance toward suicide to be supported universally, it must be based on principles more general than those of a particular religious belief. (pp. 49-52)

This article also addresses the argument that one has a duty to the human community, and in particular to the state. Aristotle opposed suicide on the grounds that it treats the state unjustly (EN 1138a 11-13) and Aquinas argued that it robs the community of one of its parts. (ST 2a2ae 64,5) As has been stated previously, in a totalitarian regime, the state's goals are paramount and override those of its citizens and may even extend to the prohibition of suicide. With this view, decisions of life and death rightfully belong to the state alone. Political traditions based on a Jeffersonian type of liberalism reverses the relationship of the individual and the state; the state is subordinate to individuals. The state exists in order to help its citizens promote their own private interests. With this theory, there is no justification for the claim that an individual has a duty to the state to continue living against his or her own wishes.

In a discussion of the fostering of moral habits, virtues and traits of character which nurture the values and goals that are esteemed by a particular culture, Moskop and Englehardt contend that it is possible to argue that a lifestyle which encourages suicide in certain circumstances tends to ignore important virtues like endurance and patience. If respect for the freedom of others is considered moral behavior, it is only proper that the pursuit of such values be with the consent of those involved. They go on to argue that an accepted practice of suicide may foster the virtues of self reliance and courage. Also, permitting suicide in certain circumstances would contribute to the general welfare of society when prolongation of life would result in great suffering for the individual and others.

Other avenues explored by the authors include the duties one owes to one's self, individual freedom (such as the Kantian argument that free will is a necessary condition for the existence of morality), and the rationality of the person who makes such a decision. It would be extremely difficult to justify the claim that all suicides are the result of mental illness, and the authors imply that such a position would preclude that there could be no life situation in which an individual might deliberately, and with good reason, choose to end his or her life. (pp. 55-56)

The only physician in our sample who brought up the question of fostering endurance and patience by not committing suicide was in practice for 39 years and was in his early seventies. He also postulated that those who were terminally ill had a duty to the community to test new medications and treatments so that others might be helped. There was only a tiny differential between Groups 1 and 2 regarding the mental stability of those wishing to commit suicide. (Over half of each group believed that mental illness was present.)

Daniel Callahan, in his book, *What Kind of Life* (1989: pp. 222-223) states that the primary argument of active euthanasia and assisted suicide has always been a relatively simple one. A dying person, or one whose life has become intolerably burdensome, has the right to request to have his or her life directly ended by another if that is necessary to avoid suffering or a hopelessly compromised existence. Alternatively, we should, with the help of others, be enabled to kill ourselves to achieve the same end. Callahan uses the popular phrase "mercy killing" to refer to the killing of one person by another as a act of kindness, not as an act of malice or self-interest on the part of the one who does the killing or assists in a suicide. As it is often said that we have a right to this kind of mercy, the author asks, "On what grounds?" His answer postulates that the moral foundation of this claimed right is that our body is our own and that our life should be subject to our self-determination. We have, he says, a right to end our own life. If we cannot accomplish this on our own, another person, may, with our permission, end it for us as an act of compassion. The law, it is argued, should recognize and sanction this possibility, with suitable procedures and safeguards to ensure a serious reason for doing so and to validate the voluntary nature of the decision. Callahan writes that the proposed legalization is important to the issue of medical allocation because it offers for many an alternative approach to the problem of the scarcity of resources and prospect of rationing. If we would simply allow people to be able to end their lives when they voluntarily choose to do so, it is said, we could simultaneously enhance determination and the conservation of resources. A powerful reason to move in that direction, Callahan argues, is the well known fact that a small minority of patients, particularly those at the end of life, consume a disproportionately large share of resources.

In the role of "Devil's Advocate," Callahan writes about the potentially harmful consequences of legalizing euthanasia. One secular argument states that making euthanasia legal would quickly get out of hand and lead to deadly abuse. He feels that this is a problematic argument since there is no clear historical evidence that abuse must always and necessarily follow legalization. The Nazi experience is not felt to be particularly relevant in this case, since Nazis did not move from legal voluntary killing to involuntary killing. What potent argument is there against euthanasia, the author queries, that does not rest exclusively on uncertain legal and social consequences but can show the intrinsic wrongfullness of euthanasia? Callahan lists them as follows: 1. It is a mistake to classify active euthanasia and assisted suicide as expressive of acts of individual autonomy. Someone else has to kill us . . . or help us kill ourselves. This is communal action; a form of social action. 2. We have never allowed killing as a form of a contractual relationship between two consenting adults. In none of the acts our society views as justified killing, is the killing for the benefit of the person killed. There must be some public interest at stake at the taking of life (war, self-defense, capital punishment). 3. Even if a case can be made for self-determination even unto death, Callahan states, "it does not follow that my right to kill myself can be transformed into the right of someone else to kill me." No human being should have the ultimate power over the fate of another.

The author goes on to state that even if we fully grant the argument that acts of euthanasia stemming from compassion and mercy can embody some commendable aspects, they are not sufficient to justify so momentous a social change. The killing of another would become a matter of individual choice and personal contract rather than societal judgment and social necessity.

Callahan tells us that it has been said that there is very little distinction between euthanasia and allowing someone to die . . . and if we grant that this is valid, what about those cases that combine an illness that renders a patient unable to breath or to eat on his/her own? If we then turn off a respirator or pull out a feeding tube . . . on the level of physical causality, have we killed the patient or allowed him/her to die? The individual who has turned off that respirator will be morally culpable if there is not a good reason to do so. That the patient has been allowed to die of his/her underlying condition does not morally excuse the one who omitted (or withdrew) those treatments. The point Callahan is making is that an intervention into a disease process does not erase the underlying disease. To accept the fact that a disease cannot be controlled after an effort has been made to do so, and treatment is then stopped, is as morally acceptable as deciding in advance that it cannot successfully be controlled. The distinction between withholding and withdrawing should be rejected for the same reason that the distinction between killing and allowing to die should be maintained; to keep clearly before us the external reality and independent causality of disease.

The author contends that physicians have come to believe that it is their choice, and their choice alone, which brings about death. They do not want to exercise that kind of authority and thus they continue to treat, feeling that if they did not continue to do so they will be causally and morally responsible for the death. They have been put in what seems to them an impossible situation. Physicians cannot be made ultimately responsible for what disease and mortality do to people. (pp. 234-237) It seems as if the burden to stop treatment is in the hands of those who want to stop treatment. Callahan feels that this is too much of a burden; the burden of proof will have to be modified. The goal is to make the patient's condition and the long term diagnosis, not the mere forestalling of death, determine the use of technology. He writes that we must, and in a very short time, change the cultural context in which we care for patients. The guidelines for this change, he says, have been polished and elaborated for over two decades in this country with far less success and impact than they deserve.

The physicians in our study were 100% in favor of life support for the elderly, and most stated that this should be on demand of the individual. Very few wanted the legal right to actively help someone to die, but as has been stated before, they were in favor of withdrawal of technology when it was no longer effective.

THE MEDICAL AND MENTAL HEALTH PROFESSIONALS

Louis S. Baer, M.D. (1978: p.32), in his book of advice to older persons, quotes an older physician's beliefs about young physicians. "They aren't old enough to have suffered long and deeply themselves. They have just seen suffering and prescribed for suffering, but have not really felt it in their bowels."

Baer goes on to state:

> My older patients are nearly unanimous in telling me that the 'real enemy' they fear is senility, or total invalidism and confinement in a nursing home, not a sudden death or a short final illness. . . . We have

perverted the Judeo-Christian tradition into a belief that biological existence, per se, is of supreme value, and on the basis of that interpretation have been side-tracked into an ethical dilemma of ghastly proportions. (Baer, p. 59)

This early supporter of the individual's right to control his/her medical destiny, committed suicide at the age of 73, ten years after the publication of his book for older persons. His wife of 51 years joined him in suicide. Dr. Baer had recently suffered a stroke; his wife had terminal cancer.

Our particular population of younger physicians was very sensitive to the issue of personal autonomy although they did not tend to have personal experience with "long and deep suffering." Biological existence, for the majority of this group, was not of paramount importance.

Thomas A. Gonda, MD, in his article "Coping with Death & Dying (1977: pp. 71-74), writes that ". . . the obligation to do everything humanly possible to preserve life gives way to one of several alternative courses of action. Of these, *benemortasia* (allowing the disease to take its course while providing only palliative symptomatic therapy, and *euthanasia* (withdrawing a regimen of treatment already begun) are the most common. The author states that, " The terminal patient is entitled to safe conduct, dignified dying and appropriate death." "Safe conduct," in this case, is the alleviation of the secondary suffering caused by the personal crisis of dying. " Dignified dying" refers to the continued regard of the dying patient as a responsible person, capable of clear perception, honest relationships, and purposeful behaviors consistent with physical decline and disability. "Appropriate death" can be defined as a death one might choose, were there a choice. Although the author does not list suicide as an alternative, his insistence that the dying patient is still capable of managing his/her own affairs (dependent on the level of compromise) leads the reader to believe that taking one's own life may be one way to achieve "appropriate death."

The older physicians in this study tended to be more positive toward "passive euthanasia." Both groups were split on the issue of deep depression arising from the experience of terminal illness leading the patient's decision to commit suicide. A large minority of both groups would agree with Gonda's discussion of the patient's ability to handle his/her own affairs during this crisis.

Walter Alvarez, MD, author of many works in the field of Suicidology, puzzles over the condemnation of the old or very ill person committing suicide in an editorial article entitled, "Is suicide by an old, dying person a sin and a crime?" (Alvarez, 1969, pp. 77-78) Alvarez feels that it is because,

> . . . the Euthanasia Society cannot hope to put over soon the idea of a doctor's deliberately helping someone like an idiot child to die. I fear that most people will object to that for a long time to come. Yet, if an old man who is dying of a very painful scattered cancer wants to end his life, I see no reason why his neighbor should say, "Hey, you can't do that; we think there is probably something in the Bible against it, and we have passed a state law against it."

The author states that "Too often I have been distressed watching well-intentioned medical friends of mine struggling day and night to keep alive for perhaps six weeks more . . . a patient who is riddled with cancer and begging to be left alone." Alvarez recounts a conversation with an elderly patient. "As one such old man said to me, 'Suppose you keep me alive--or what? I have no family, no place to go, no hope of ever a job again. I am here to die, and I want to get the job over with as quickly as possible.'" To his dismay, Alvarez' medical friends kept this man alive as long as possible ". . . because of some weird and supposed Hippocratic idea."

This piece was written over 20 years ago, and although extreme medical measures are no longer routinely undertaken, the idea of helping a patient to die, as we know, is still being hotly debated. As has been already stated, our two groups of physicians were not in favor of helping a patient to die. However, it was not the Hippocratic Oath that prevented this type of intervention, according to the respondents, but a combination of personal morality and the physician's oath.

Physicians Shirley Bromberg and Christine Cassel approach the dilemma in an article debating the limits of paternalism when treating the elderly. (Bromberg & Cassel, Vol.31, no. 11, pp. 698-703) The authors discuss Thomas Szasz's views on suicidal thoughts; they are not symptoms of a disease, and therefore the individual should not be coerced into treatment. The public should not properly interfere with the suicide since it is an action primarily affecting the self. Bromberg & Cassel state that:

> Others would argue that except in terminal illness, there is no such thing as a 'rational suicide.' Despair and depression, which usually contribute to the act of suicide, rob one's intellectual abilities and distort one's outlook for the future. Those who would prohibit all suicides say that one can never know what lies in the future; a seemingly hopeless situation may be radically altered if one is prevented from acting drastically in a moment of despair. (pp. 698-703)

Suicidologists base their rationale for suicide prevention on this notion, according to the authors. Suicidologists claim the suicidal person is in the middle of an acute crisis and is highly ambivalent, and they argue that a suicidal crisis may be only a momentary aberration, lasting minutes or hours. The authors counter this with evidence that the aged person who contemplates suicide is less ambivalent and more likely to use a method that does not permit intervention and rescue. (ie: guns, autocide, etc.) The future, they state, is unlikely to improve while suffering from chronic or severe illness. Under such pressures, with little hope of improvement, an older person may rationally choose to terminate his life prematurely, as supported by Barrington in *Apologia for Suicide*:

> Death taken in one's own time and with a sense of purpose, may in fact be far more bearable than the process of waiting to be arbitrarily extinguished . . . A lot of kindly people may feel that this is lacking in respect for the honorable estate of old age; but to insist on the obligation of old people to live through a period of decline and helplessness seems to me to be lacking in a feeling for the demands of human self- respect." (Barrington, 1976, pp. 396-401)

In discussing the ethics of the problem, Bromberg and Cassel feel that the conflict can be posed in terms of two broad ethical principles which underlie the problem: beneficence and respect for autonomy. "Beneficence" refers to doing good, or to acting in accord with the golden rule. Respect for persons includes a sense of their independence and requires a recognition of their rights and desires for self-determination. In issues of mental health, especially with the elderly, these two principles often seem to conflict. For example, in certain circumstances, when an old person refuses to accept help, this may be viewed as an act of pride which is to be respected under the principle of autonomy. However, if the person is depressed, confused, or has a psychiatric disorder, often it is felt that the person cannot decide for himself and that he/she needs intervention. The person's emotional state may itself be considered to be life-threatening, just as depression manifested itself as a suicide attempt. As such, depression and despair are symptoms of mental illness. But if patients are viewed as sick when suicidal, they are necessarily also viewed as incompetent and considered incapable of making appropriate decisions. The medical model implies that treatment is possible, likely to be effective, and therefore, warranted. With these assumptions, not to treat is abandonment or neglect. Thus the principle of beneficence can lead to attitudes of paternalism, and to health professionals undertaking to intervene coercively or deceptively in the life of a person for "his or her own good." The authors go on to state that an advocate of paternalism might argue that the world is so complicated that the abilities and skills of the geriatric age group are inadequate or obsolete, therefore, they need assistance. Similar arguments are made for mental patients. Paternalism uses beneficence as its justification but it diverges from pure beneficence in one significant respect: paternalists not only act in someone else's interest, but may do so in opposition to that individuals expressed wishes. The authors advise physicians to protect the individual's right to self-determination, and to continued involvement with the patient . . . since the majority of elderly people will visit their primary care physician shortly before their suicide. The physician may need to accept the uncertainty about the appropriateness of his or her decision. Moral dilemmas often provoke feelings of discomfort, for they often require a choice between two unsatisfactory options: institutionalizing the elderly person (as in a genuine emergency with no opportunity to assess the person's state of mind), or respecting the decision of a mentally clear and rational individual to refuse treatment.

Clearly, our population of younger physicians are struggling with the paternalism issue. The older physician's attitudes seem to reflect something else; perhaps a relationship with the patient that is affected by contemporaneity. It is perhaps more difficult to distance one's self from suffering if your patient is in your own age range, and the unconscious (or conscious) identification with that patient creates a barrier to accepting personal autonomy with regard to suicide; this constitutes a major defeat for some physicians.

Mansell E. Pattison, in his book devoted to the experience of dying (Pattison, 1977, pp. 14-16), discusses other kinds of professional distortions. He writes about the adoption of logical, rigid patterns of the progress of dying so that doctors can follow scientific course of action. In his words, dying is made acceptable by professional objectification. Many physicians identify with the dying, and may seek to undo past guilts, or their own death anxieties. "This vicarious identification is also a defense, for the miraculous occurs . . . for the dying person is dead, I am still alive." Therefore, dying is also made acceptable through professional subjectification.

Mansell quotes Robert Lifton in order to place this existential dilemma in socio-historical context:

> In every age man faces a pervasive theme which defies his engagement and yet must be engaged. In Freud's day it was sexuality and moralism. Now it is technological violence and absurd death. We do well to name the threat and analyze its components. (p. 8)

Mansell feels that death accepting attitudes place death in perspective as a part of life and integral to existence, and quotes Cappon's view that favoring euthanasia is a "psychologically desired attitude toward life and death." (p. 291) Evidence stated for this judgment is the fact that fear of death is greater among patients with psychiatric illnesses than among patients with physical illness or non-patients, and psychiatric patients are least in favor of euthanasia. Bringing in an Eriksonian perspective, he points out that "What must be explored is the etiology of such attitudes--and the extent to which euthanasia is related to other indices of 'ontegrity' in the older person but is not related to indices of despair." (Erikson, 1963)

Again, it is necessary to state that a majority of both groups of physicians studied believed that mental illness, probably in the form of depression, was present if suicide was contemplated. Depression was given as a cause of suicidal ideation, and not the underlying losses, etc., that create despair.

Robert Kastenbaum discusses the conflicting attitudes toward the elderly that affect professional judgement. He states that physicians' attitudes toward aging and death are likely to affect terminal care of the aged:

> If we are convinced it is right or necessary for an old person to die, then we may be making it extraordinarily difficult for him to live. We may fail to bolster his chances of remaining in good health, we may fail to recognize when, in fact, his pre-terminal process has begun, and we may remain so closeted in our own assumptions that we do not bother to find out what he really needs in his last hours. (Kastenbaum, 1972, pp. 116-125)

Our younger physicians, again, were more likely to believe that there is an inherent right to die, approved of suicide for the terminally ill, and were more accepting of family help in suicide.

THE CLERGY AND PROFESSIONAL ADVOCATES

As stated previously, while discussing the "Right to Die Laws" during the First Euthanasia Conference, Nov. 23, 1968, the *Reverend Robert B. Reeves, Jr.* stated that ". . . they do not directly address the slowly progressive, chronic, totally incapacitating medical diseases of the heart, kidneys, lungs, brain, and liver—the vital organs." He explained that since these laws are only applicable in the terminal two weeks of one's life, they are of no help in avoiding months or years in a nursing home. (in Baer, 1978, p. 108)

While our younger respondents did not state that in certain cases it is right or necessary for an old person to die, the majority was more approving of suicide for this age group, especially those suffering from terminal illness.

Derek Humphrey and Ann Wickett, co-founders of The Hemlock Society of Los Angeles, look at history and demographics to understand euthanasia. (Humphrey & Wickett, 1986) They quote Herodotus (c.485-c.425 BCE) in the statement, "When life is so burdensome, death has become for man a sought-after-refuge." Humphrey and Wickett point out that what we once asked for from physicians in a pre-technological era has changed considerably, especially for those who are elderly or are suffering from terminal illness or degenerative diseases that do not kill, but totally incapacitate the individuals. The authors state, "The cry, save me doctors, has turned to save me from machines, Doctor." As this was not forthcoming, especially for those without a terminal condition,

> Mercy killings rose ten times in the 1980's compared to any five-year period since 1920, while murder-suicide, double suicides, and assisted suicides involving the terminally ill increased forty times as desperate elderly people felt obliged to take the law and fate into their own hands. (1986:xi)

Medicine caters to the biological man, according to Humprey and Wickett, often abandoning the psychological and social one. "Pneumonia, formerly the 'old man's friend' is treated with antibiotics. The patient lingers-often in pain." (xi)

Ann Humphrey Wickett, suffering from breast cancer, committed suicide in 1991. It is not known if this was a treatable or terminal illness.

The physicians in this study were 100% in favor of life support for the elderly, often because the patient or the family requested the measure. While they tended to reserve the right to terminate "extraordinary means" to keep a patient alive, no concrete guidelines were offered for this act.

THE ELDERLY

Writing from the perspective of an older woman, *Doris Portwood* challenges the current religious, medical and legal aspects of suicide. In her overview of history, she cites the early Christian dogma against suicide as a response to unrestrained and unnecessary martyrdom. She also points out that the Hebrew Bible does not take a moral stance on suicide, but reports the actions of those who "fell upon their swords." In this way, Portwood negates the religious attitude that suicide is a "historical" sin. (Portwood, 1978, pp. 11-14) Portwood confronts the problem of mental status, and she quotes *Webster's Collegiate Dictionary* as saying, "Suicide is the act or an instance of taking one's own life voluntarily and intentionally especially by a person of years of discretion and of sound mind." (p. 15) As the conflict continues over what is a "sound mind," one is aware that Portwood has side-stepped an important issue . . . according to Webster, there is no suicide if a sound mind is absent. Following this premise, that mental stability is present, Portwood suggests that the horror of a "botched" suicide be avoided by the incorporation of how-to information along with counseling at suicide prevention centers. The author feels that these professionals could be trained to ascertain an older person's mental status and be able to winnow out those who cannot make an informed decision. (p. 98) She counsels those wishing to commit suicide to pre-plan; the obtaining of information from physicians and pharmacists on dosage levels without compromising their ethics, and the need to be acquainted with one's own tolerance for various chemicals. The author also addresses the concept of euthanasia, and the avoidance of legal retribution for helpers.

An especially important point made by Portwood, that should effect the way we look at statistics, is that women, who attempt suicide more than men, are less successful in their attempts. This should not lead researchers to believe that these women are not as serious in their attempts. The author believes that lack of information and male-oriented weaponry, including the physical strength for implementation contributes to this skewed result. She also states that women also tend to want to leave a more presentable corpse for others to find, protecting others' sensibilities, and this leads to non-violent, but less effective means. (pp. 76-78)

Most of our sample of physicians appear to be against giving "lethality information" to their patients. However, the monitoring of certain types of medication should create an awareness of stockpiling. In not refusing to renew these drugs, the physician may be making an unconscious (or unintended) statement confirming personal autonomy with regard to suicide.

THE FAMILY CAREGIVER

Betty Rollin (1985), defying the medical establishment and the legal system, has written a heart-rending book about her mother's assisted death. (A film by Rollin, based on this book, was aired on national television.)

Rollin's mother, dying from incurable cancer in her late seventies, could no longer physically or mentally continue her chemotherapy treatments . . . even though all of her physicians insisted that she would have a better prognosis if she did. Wracked by nausea and pain, with no real hope of recovery, Mrs. Rollin begged to die, but was ignored by doctors who either feared for their licenses, or were holding on to the idea of life at all costs, even life without quality and full of pain. The author's search for an answer to her mother's dilemma, and her own journey toward acceptance of loss gives us a unique view of the stresses and rewards of caregiving for the terminally ill. Eventually, a foreign physician known for his views regarding suicide and active or passive euthanasia, gave Rollin the information she needed to acquire the proper dosages of medication, and make it available to her mother if she wished to use it. Rollin's mother died peacefully in her own bed, in her own time, and by her own hand. This story is one of personal control and autonomy in the face of impossible odds and incredible agony; agony that many physicians, according to the author, cannot even begin to comprehend, but must now begin to address.

Most physicians were aware at the time of their interview that Dr. Jack Kervorkian was embroiled in several legal battles for making his "Suicide Machine" available to several people who wanted to end their own lives without having to ask family members to be the instrument of death. The giving of information may be construed as lethal as providing the means, and our sample of doctors showed a very low acceptance rate for physicians to provide this care, and most physicians were against the legalization of this kind of help.

VI
Epilogue

A REASONED RESPONSE

During the 1966 October term of the Supreme Court of the United States, The American Geriatrics Society presented, as *Amicus Curiae* ("friend of the court"), a brief urging the reversal of several judgments that would allow individual States power to engage "in any activity that their citizens choose for the common weal, no matter how unorthodox or unnecessary anyone else, including the judiciary, deems state involvement to be." In simpler terms, The Society, made up of 6,000 professional care providers, argued against allowing States to legalize physician assisted suicide. (PAS) The arguments put forward included everything from the misperception of death experience to the moral and medical dilemmas facing physicians with patients requesting an end to their perceived suffering.

According to the Society, legalization of PAS would create a moral dilemma for geriatricians in that they would be collaborating in causing early death for those in disadvantaged situations. This would make them complicit in a social policy which eliminates those most in need of services in order to conserve public funds. They also urged a continued debate on the merits of PAS, since improving life at its end stage has only just become the focus of research and innovation.

MISPERCEPTIONS OF END-OF LIFE EXPERIENCES

It is postulated that there are three serious misperceptions that the courts relied on in overturning state laws prohibiting PAS as unconstitutional. The first misperception postulates that the courts were misinformed as to how people actually live during the process of dying and the case histories of those cited in the plaintiff's cases did not represent the usual situation of persons facing death. The named patients all had a single, well-defined disease such as AIDS or cancer. In advanced old age, there are multiple conditions and uncertain prognoses to contend with. The average age of the plaintiff-patient was 56 years. None of the plaintiffs were as old as the median age of death in the U.S.; 77 years. None was characterized as without family, living in a nursing home or poor. They all had physicians and none mentioned inadequate health insurance. Statistics show that the illnesses that our elderly tend to succumb to include cancer, heart disease, organ system failure and dementia; these ordinarily cause progressive disability over more than a year. Prognosis is uncertain and poverty and isolation is common. One in five of our elderly citizens dies in a nursing home. Psychiatric problems and depression are largely unrecognized and go untreated. The court was asked to imagine, rather than the plaintiff's dilemma, the much more real ". . . elderly widow who is blind, nearly deaf, disabled, and in a Medicaid nursing home." The median life expectancy is 79 for women and 72 for men in 1996. Those surviving to age 65 will have a median age at death 80 for men and 84 for women making the nursing home resident's plight a distinct possibility for many of our elderly.

The lower court characterized dying as unavoidably dreadful with severe and protracted suffering and contrasts this with assisted suicide which lets a patient die with dignity. The geriatricians argued that most people die quietly in their sleep and that hospice and palliative care have been able to relieve pain for most of their patients without substantial sedation. Also, it is already permissible to give aggressive palliative care such as heavy sedation and withdrawal of life support when a patient is very near the end of life. (It was admitted in the brief that the standard of care lags behind what may be achieved due to barriers against the availability of certain narcotics and a delay in the adoption of better medical decisions by health care professionals.)

In an article for The Detroit Free Press (1996,) author Suzanne Gordon states that "In the United States, palliative care and hospice pioneers have demonstrated that there is more to medicine than curing disease and defeating death. But their work is one of the best kept secrets in America." She goes on to say that ". . . when it comes to the care of the chronically and terminally ill, most physicians in this country are as ignorant as their patients." The geriatricians make the claim that the current shortcomings in "end of life care" are not "persistent" or "unchanging." The impact of managed care on the provision of services for those with poor prognoses is not yet clear, but more and more of those patients whose chance for survival is small, are electing to forgo life-sustaining treatment.

PAS IS NO DIFFERENT THAN FOREGOING LIFE SUPPORT

The American Geriatrics Society defines PAS as when the physician ". . . provides either equipment or medication, or informs the patient of the most efficacious use of already available means, for the sole purpose of assisting the patient to end his or her own life." The foregoing of life sustaining treatment (FLST) is defined as the point at which intervention is either not supplied or the on-going use of the intervention is discontinued, letting the underlying disease state to progress to a natural conclusion. There are moral differences between the two situations, as well as practical issues such as access to medical care, clinical intent and decision-making processes. (It is noted that many individuals think about suicide or wish for pre-emptive death when they are angry or suffering.) FLST decisions come into effect when life-sustaining treatment is unwarranted. In the case of PAS, fear of suffering or losing dignity, as well as controlling the circumstances of their demise may prompt a person to make a plea for assistance in dying before suffering has become unbearable. In doing so, patients may be robbing themselves of valuable time to be with their families or to get their affairs in order. Good palliative care, the organization states, ". . . aims to eliminate the suffering, whereas PAS succeeds only be eliminating the sufferer." It is also matter of law that failure to remove or withhold FLST against the patient's wishes is an *unconsented touching*, better known as "battery." Leaving a patient alone is clearly different than imposing death from drug overdose.

As already noted, the plaintiffs sought PAS for a limited class of persons: terminally ill, competent, acting voluntarily and suffering. All legislation today includes these caveats. This highlights the fact that PAS is considered differently by its proponents, the law, the care providers and the public in general. Therefore, it is argued that the assumption by the courts regarding the equity of these "courses of treatment" is not based on reality and should not be used as an argument for PAS.

CONSTRAINTS PROPOSED FOR PAS PRESENT INTRACTACTABLE PROBLEMS

Two circuit courts found there was a constitutional right to PAS based on the restrictive criteria mentioned throughout this chapter; ie: the terminally ill, mentally competent, those suffering from severe pain and make a voluntary request for PAS. As these decisions were based on erroneous assumptions, the American Geriatrics Society states that if PAS was implemented, determination of eligibility would be "intractably difficult," and the constraints put in place would likely fail to achieve the desired effect of safeguarding those at risk for inappropriate intervention. *The Uniform Rights of the Terminally Ill Act* and over 40 state natural death statutes show "terminal illness" is very difficult to define and the definition of "terminally ill" for hospice or advance directive measures has been very problematic. The drafters of the Uniform Act omits any reference to terminal condition and does not attempt to define terminal illness. Since the legislation in question is partially based on the Uniform Rights act, these standards cannot hold before legal scrutiny. They do, however, beg for a more rigorous definition of terminal illness. Subjective determination should be made based on all factors in an individual's case. This changes the strategy of correcting abnormality with long survival expected, to one of stabilizing function, giving physical comfort, and providing emotional support for the dying patient.

Statistical determination of terminal illness with an explicit threshold encounters serious barriers. Very little research addresses this issue and most people will die of diseases that are not predictable with a statistical model. There is no justifiable reason to set the threshold at any particular point. A specific threshold is inconsistent with known data; most persons dying of chronic organ system failure would not meet the threshold of predefined terminal conditions and many patients with opportunity for treatment and "prolonged survival" would find themselves encompassed within the threshold. As the prognosis for survival may depend on options and availability of treatment, as well as patient and physician choice, the "terminally ill" status is uncomfortably dependent on volitional actions rather than the status of the patient.

A very important point made in this brief against adoption of PAS is one of competence. Cognitive failure is commonplace in severe illness. These deficits change over time and not often detected in usual care situations. Depression is common and also under-detected and untreated. If the right to PAS extends only to those patients with "contemporaneous competence," those with disease states that tend to lead to incompetence may elect to die early. This is a risk with those patients who suffer from early dementia; patients understand what is happening at the moment, but have a failing memory. The worse case scenario postulated by the geriatricians is one in which a person may sacrifice many relatively comfortable and capable years out of fear of future incompetency.

Coercion within the context of care is also problematic. Voluntary choice without undue influence projects the image of an independently functioning person evaluating his or her options, unaffected by biased individuals or other circumstances. As this is far from the usual experience of dying, the organization postulates that physical incapacity, emotional lability and vulnerability to financial and family constraints, as well as availability of appropriate health care, may result in inappropriate requests for PAS.

Today's medical practice has no consensus on the definition or the measurement of "suffering." PAS would be limited to those who are suffering or in pain. As pain control is already available without any change in the existing law, it is difficult for these geriatricians to see why death through PAS is a better, and possibly constitutionally dictated, option.

PHYSICIAN INVOLVEMENT

The American Geriatrics Society states that there is no reason to believe that today's doctors have expertise in all modes of "killing," yet all proposals for PAS mandate physician involvement. There is no drug that is approved as safe and effective, no instruction in medical texts, and practice standards show widespread inattention to counseling and symptom management for those who are dying. According to Suzanne Gordon (1996), *The Cecil Textbook of Medicine* used by most medical students devotes only three of its 2,300 pages to the care of terminally ill patients. She goes on to state that "Only 17 percent of the nation's accredited medical residency programs offer training in hospices; less than 9 percent of these rotations are required."

In her book, *Last Rites: Death Control and the Elderly in America,* Barbara J. Logue reiterates that medical education focused on the care of the dying patient has long been inadequate despite the increase of our aging population. "A recent survey of schools for medical, nursing and social works students found 'no evidence of a consensus on the need for death education for health professionals.'" No evidence was found of the development of course content or approach to the dying and no evidence was found of any attempt to integrate training to facilitate team care in this area. (1993, pp. 235-236)

Due to the arguments discussed in the brief, The American Geriatrics Society stated unequivocally that "This Court should reverse the opinions of the lower courts, and decline to recognize a constitutional right to PAS for a limited class of persons at the end of life." (Brief of the American Geriatrics Society, No. 95-1858, No. 96-110, in the Supreme Court of the United States, October term, 1996, pp. 1-20)

The Society's brief was cited three times in the oral arguments in January of 1997. Before the ruling, Dr. Joanne Lynn, a representative of the Society, reported in personal correspondence to this author, that letters of thanks from the attorneys general were received and indications that the presence of the American Geriatrics Society made an impact on the court and the protagonists involved.

THE RULING

On Thursday, June 26, the Supreme Court ruled that individual states may *continue to ban* the practice of physician assisted suicide (PAS). In a 9-0 decision, various justices suggested that, in the future, some terminally ill persons in intractable pain *may* be able to claim a constitutional right to a physician's assistance in hastening death.

Chief Justice William Rehnquist stated in the court's principal ruling, "Our opinion does not absolutely foreclose such a claim." One of the four other justices who signed the opinion, Justice Sandra Day O'Connor, said that even though she agreed that there was no "generalized" right to commit suicide, she still held as an open question, the right of a "mentally competent person who is experiencing great suffering" that cannot be made in any way tolerable, has a constitutionally based "interest in controlling the circumstances of his or her imminent death"

The court's tone seemed to be matching that of the American Geriatrics Society; a thoughtful step forward in the quest for a solution that will redefine the limits of governmental interference and promote individual freedom. Rehnquist stated, reminiscent of the Society's plea, ". . . throughout the nation, Americans are engaged in earnest and profound debate about the morality, legality and practicality of physician assisted suicide." He noted that the court's approach ". . . permits this debate to continue, as it should in a democratic society." There was, however, an explicit discussion in a concurring opinion by Justice David Souter, that individual states could experiment and permit physician assisted suicide if they chose to do so. He stated that the court should ". . . stay its hand to allow reasonable legislative consideration."

It is thought that the fairly inconclusive ruling was a result of the question of whether a right to physician assisted suicide should be seen as an aspect of the "liberty" that is protected by the 14th Amendment's guarantee of due process; a reframing of the argument on behalf of the aforementioned non-geriatric, terminally ill patients. Rehnquist stated that the due process clause does not include a right to commit suicide with another person's assistance. The factors that were the most relevant, he indicated, was a seven hundred year aversion and disapproval of suicide and assisted suicide in the "Anglo-American legal tradition; the considered policy of almost every state; and strong governmental interests in protecting the vulnerable and avoiding the "path to voluntary and perhaps even involuntary euthanasia."

It is interesting to note that the case made for the distinction between assisting suicide and withdrawing life-sustaining treatment by the Society was upheld by Rehnquist. He stated that it is ". . . a distinction widely recognized and endorsed in the medical profession and in our legal traditions, and is both important and logical. It is certainly rational."

Some Concluding Remarks

The elderly are living longer and seem to be demanding more and more care from a society that has found itself fending off the specter of death, refusing to let go or give up if the means can be found to "maintain." By maintain, I refer to the use of life support without the possibility of cure, or even the amelioration of a long standing condition. However, those elders may not be the ones asking for these supposed miracles. It may be the children who are influenced by their longing for a non-existent "golden age," or the professional caregivers who may not be able to let go of symbolic parents or grandparents. Can this society let our elders go when they are mentally and physically ready? The physicians in this preliminary study of attitude appear to be of two minds—the younger group embracing new philosophies rather than new technology, and the group with the most years in practice clinging to technology and rejecting the "new" humanism. Perhaps the patient of the future will be more aware of the personal beliefs of their chosen caregiver, so that the original historical contract between patient and clinician, rather than the force of law, will again be the cornerstone of medical practice.

Bertrand Russell writes in *Portraits from Memory*,

> An individual's human existence should be like a river--small at first, narrowly contained within its banks, and rushing passionately past boulders and over waterfalls. Gradually, the river grows wider, the banks recede, the waters flow more quietly, and in the end, without any visible break, they become merged in the sea, and painlessly lose their individual being. (1956, Simon & Shuster: New York)

This is a wonderfully romantic view, and I believe that most of our elderly would welcome this "oneness" with creation if given the chance. The reality for many, however, is constant physical and psychic collisions with the rocks onshore. To have a good death, if one cannot embrace life, has been an historical quest. Can this society help our elders to make a good escape, if in their frailty the rocks hold them captive along the shore? I cannot answer for society, only report what is happening at this stage of our social evolution with regard to the embrace of death by those who are unwilling to live. I am heartened by the discussion and the controversy, for this is the foundation of new knowledge. Perhaps, when I am ready to depart for my next adventure, and join my ancestors in whatever realm that may exist . . . the fear of death in this society will have lessened enough for us to take charge of our passing.

Lori Secouler
June, 1997

Appendix A
Sample Letter to Physicians

July 17, 1990

Dr. ————
333 N. Oxford Valley Road
Fairless Hills, PA 19030

Dear Dr.————,

As a concerned physician, you are well aware of the ever increasing number of attempted, and successful suicides in our area. During my Ph.D. program in Clinical Psychology, I will be addressing this problem, and I will be focusing on the general practitioner's knowledge, concerns and pro-posed treatment for those at risk.

My research will be limited to general medical practices in Bucks County, and I believe your particular insight would be beneficial to my understanding of the subject, the final product of which will be a major paper and possible textbook.

I would very much appreciate your putting aside a small amount of your valuable time to meet with me, at your convenience, to discuss the general practitioner's thoughts regarding suicide. I will call your office within the next two weeks to schedule our meeting. Since I am unable to financially reimburse you for your time, I will be happy to send you the results of the study, and any other publications arising from your participation. (The interview takes approximately 20 minutes)

Thank you in advance for your most valuable assistance. I am,

Sincerely yours,

Lori M. Secouler

Appendix B
Likert Scale Question Pool

Attitudes Re: Elderly

People over 65 should have special discounts and services just because of their age.

The elderly should not be segregated in their living arrangements.

Old people should be allowed to commit suicide if they are in pain.

Senior citizens take up too much of the US health care dollar.

People over 65 should retire so that younger workers can have a chance.

The elderly are given too much attention in the media.

Old people should never be placed on life support.

Senior citizens take up too much of my energy in private practice.

The elderly do not have a lot of emotional problems.

Senility is a normal part of old age.

Old people are not as depressed as other age groups.

Anxiety is a normal part of growing older.

More old people should consider suicide if they are in poor health.

Old people should consider suicide as an alternative to entering a nursing home.

Geriatric medicine must be a very depressing specialty.

Medicare should be available on a "financial need" basis, the same as Medicaid.

It is not profitable to rehabilitate an elderly stroke patient.

Families of the elderly are given enough help to keep them at home.

Physicians should help an elderly person to die peacefully, instead of having to deal with terminal illness.

Poverty is not a concern for today's elderly.

Good medical care for the aged is not dependent on their personal finances.

More elderly people should commit suicide, whatever the reason.

Most aged people become dependent.

The general population is unaware of elder suicide.

The medical profession is unaware of the etiology of elder suicide. Most people think it is OK for an elderly person to take his own life. Old people, on the whole, have little to contribute to society.

I feel better about passive suicide of the elderly than I do about euthanasia.

It is OK for family members to help an old person to die.

I have trouble talking about death to my patients.

Appendix C
Actual Questions Used in Study

1. How long have you been in practice?
2. How would you characterize the population you are treating? i.e.: What percentage pediatric, adolescent, adult, geriatric? Age is geriatric??
3. Have you ever had a patient commit suicide while you were treating them?
4. While you were not actively treating them?
5. If yes/ how old were they?
6. Violent means/passive means?
7. In your estimation, which age group is most at risk?
8. Why?
9. If Dr. did not state the elderly ask the following: Are you aware of the high incidence of elder suicide?
10. If yes, where did you acquire this awareness?
11. How do you feel about elderly suicide as compared to other age groups?
12. How would you treat an elderly suspected suicide, as compared to another age group. Medication? Hospitalization?
13. If an elderly person was physically well, but still wanted to commit suicide . . . how would you view this? Mental illness? Sanity?
14. Are you aware of the cues to elder suicide?
15. Have you ever asked a person point-blank if they were contemplating suicide? An elderly person?

16. Would you approve of suicide ror a terminally ill person? An older person? a younger person?

17. How do you feel about family members helping someone to commit suicide? A young person? An old person?

18. Should it be legal for a physician to help someone die if that is their wish? A young person? An old person?

19. Do you feel better about passive suicide . . . the refusal of nourishment and medication . . . than an active attempt?

20. Do you think that there is a sex and race differential in elder suicide?

21. Do you feel comfortable in your skills in assessing immediate suicide risk?

22. Would you be afraid to ask about suicide plans with a depressed elderly patient for fear of giving him/her ideas? A younger person? Have you ever done it?

23. What do you feel might be the prime motivation for an elderly person to attempt suicide?

24. Have you ever had a specific geriatric medicine classes in medical school? Did they discuss suicide?

25. Does anyone have the right to take their own life?

26. How do you feel about life-support for the elderly?

27. Are your attitudes regarding suicide due to your personal morality, or to your training and oath as a physician?

28. Would you like to clarify any of your statements. . . or add something I have missed, or you feel is important?

Appendix D
Cues to Elder Suicide

1. Clinical Depression due to recent bereavement, financial problems or role loss.
2. Apathy and social withdrawal.
3. A prior attempt at suicide.
4. Statement of intent to commit suicide.
5. Isolation from friends and family during physical or emotional problems, possibly due to distance or absence of significant others.
6. Patient puts his/her affairs in order and/or makes funeral arrangements.
7. Abnormal rate of renewal for potentially lethal medication.
8. Increased use of alcohol.
9. Emotional distress due to real or imagined major illness, or to intractable functional or somatic pain.
10. Discussion of suicide methods with others and/or the purchase of suicide related objects, ie: material from the Hemlock Society, guns, etc.
11. Refusal of food and medication in an attempt to "passively" end life.

Adapted from Secouler, L. & Tronetti, P. (1989) p.22

Appendix E

Leading Causes of Depression in the Elderly Population

Physical changes

1. Decreased serotonin levels.
2. Decreased norepinephrine levels.
3. Increased monoamine oxidase levels.

Physical causes

1. Side effects of medication.
2. Malnutrition.
3. Alzheimer's disease.
4. Cancer (early sign)

Sociological aspects

1. Lack of control over decision-making.
2. Failing health.
3. Death of a spouse.
4. Loss of a job, independence, income.
5. Loss of home, mobility.

Adapted from Secouler, L. & Tronetti, P. (1989) p.22

Bibliography

Alvarez, W. "Is suicide by an old, dying person a sin and a crime?" in *Geriatrics, October 1969.*

American Geriatrics Society, (1996*) Brief of the American Geriatrics Society as Amicus Curiae Urging Reversal of the Judgments of the Court of Appeals for the Second Circuit Court, State of Washington and the Court of Appeals for the Ninth Circuit Court.* Presented to the Supreme Court of the United States, October Term, (No. 95-1858, No. 96-110)

Aquinas, St. Thomas (1929) *The "Summa Theologica" of Saint Thomas Aquinas, X,* translated by the Fathers of the Dominican Province. London: Furns, Oates and Washbourne.

Aristotle (1953) *The Ethics of Aristotle.* Harmondsworth, England: Penguin Books.

Atchley, R. (1960) *The Social Forces in Later Life.* Belmont, California: Wadsworth, Inc.

Baer, L. (1978) *Let the Patient Decide: A Doctor's Advice to Older Persons.* Philadelphia: Westminster Press.

Barrington, M. (1976) "Apologia for suicide," in Gorovitz, et. al. (eds.) *Moral Problems in Medicine.* Englewood Cliffs, NJ: Prentice-Hall.

Batchelor, I. & Napier, M. (1963) "Attempting Suicide in Old Age," *British Medical Journal, No. 2.*

Birren, J. & Schaie, K. (Eds.) (1985) *Handbook of the Psychology of Aging,* 2ed., Van Nostrand Rheinhold Co., Inc., New York.

Bromberg, S. & Cassel, C. "Suicide in the Elderly: The Limits of Paternalism." in *Journal of American Geriatrics Society, Vol. 31, No. 11.*

Busse, E. & Pfeiffer, E. (1969) *Behavior and Adaptation in Later Life.* Boston: Little Brown.

Callahan, D. (1989) *What Kind of Life: The Limits of Medical Progress.* New York: Simon & Schuster.

Charles, A. & DeAnfrasio, R. (1970) *The History of Hair: An Illustrated Review of Hair Fashions for Men Throughout the Ages.* New York: Bonanza Books.

Comfort, A. (1976) *A Good Age.* New York: Crown Publishers, Inc.

Conwell, Yeates (1996) *Suicide Among Older People.* Produced for American Foundation for Suicide Prevention Southeast through an unrestricted grant from Solvay Phramaceuticals, Inc.

Donne, J. (1930) *Biathanatos* (reprint of 1st ed., 1644). New York: Facsimile Text Society.

Dorpat, T. & Boswell, J. (1980) "An Evaluation of Suicidal Intent and Suicidal Attempts" in Zarit, Steven H., *Aging and Mental Disorders,* The Free Press, New York.

Durkheim, E. (1897) *Le Suicide.* (reprint, 1912 - Spaulding & Simpson, translators, 1957 ed.) New York: The Free Press of Glencoe.

Erikson, J., Erikson E. & Kivnik, H. (1986) *Vital Involvement in Old Age.* New York: W. W. Norton & Co.

Evans, G. & Farberow, N. (1988) *The Encyclopedia of Suicide,* Facts on File, New York .

Fanning, O. (1996) *"Internal Medicine World Report"* Washington Report, July 1996.

Farberow, N. (1975) *Suicide in Different Cultures.* Baltimore: University Park Press.

Fedden, R. (1938) *Suicide: A Social and Historical Study.* London: Peter Davies.

Fischer, D. (1978) *Growing Old in America.* (expanded ed.) New York: Oxford University Press.

Freud, S. (1959) "The Predisposition to Obsessional Neurosis." in Strachey, J. (ed.), *Collected Papers* New York: Basic Books.

Goffman, E. (1963) *Stigma: Notes on the Management of Spoiled Identity.* Englewood Cliffs, NJ: Prentice-Hall.

Gonda, T. "Coping with Death & Dying" *Stanford Seminar in Geriatrics, Sept. 1977.*

Gordon, S. (1996) "Doctors Mistreat Patients with Deathbed Manners" in the *Detroit News, October 18, 1996 issue.*

Haber, C. (1983) *Beyond Sixty-Five: The Dilemma of Old Age in America's Past.* New York: Cambridge University Press.

Hankoff, L. (1979) "Judaic Origins of the Suicide Prohibition" in *Suicide-Theory and Clinical Aspects*, Hankoff, L. D. & Einsidler, B. (eds.) Littleton, MA: PSG Publishing.

———— (1979) " A First Century A.D. View of Suicide: Flavius Josephus" in *Suicide: Theory and Clinical Aspects*. Hankoff, L.D. and Einsidler, B. (eds.) Littleton, MA: PSG.

Herodotus. (485-425 BCE) *Vol. 1, Book 11*, Chapters 1-98.

Humphrey D. & Wickett, A. (1986) *The Right to Die: Understanding Euthanasia.* New York: Harper & Row.

Isaac, S. & Michael W. (1982) *Handbook on Research and Evaluation.* (2 ed.) San Diego: EdITS publishers.

Kastenbaum, R. (1972) "While the Old Man Dies: Our Conflicting Attitudes Toward the Elderly," in Schoenberg, B, Carr, A. et al (eds.) *Psychosocial Aspects of Terminal Care.* New York: Columbia University Press.

Kybalova, L., Herbenova, O. & Lamarova, M. (1968) *The Pictorial Encyclopedia of Fashion.* New York: Crown Publishers, Inc.

Logue, B. (1993) *Last Rites: Death Control and the Elderly in America,* New York: Lexington Books.

McIntosh, J., Santos, J., Hubbard, R. & Overholser, J. (1996) *The Suicide of Older Men and Women,* (Sept. 11, 1996) copyright, Carol Lindemann for CyberPsych, ttp://www.cyberpsych.org/

Melamed, E. (1983) *Mirror, Mirror: The Terror of Not Being Young. New York*: Linden Press/Simon & Shuster.

Miller, M. (1979) " Toward A Profile of the Older White Male Suicide" in Miller, M., *Suicide After Sixty,* Springer Publishing Co., New York.

———— (1979) *Suicide After Sixty-The Final Alternative,* Springer Publishing Co., New York.

More, T. (1516) *Utopia.* (1981 ed. trans. by Paul Turner) New York: Penguin Books.

Moskop, J. & Englehardt, H. "The Ethics of Suicide: A Secular View" in *Suicide: Theory & Clinical Aspects*, 1979; Hankoff, L. & Einsidler, B. (eds.) Littleton, MA: PSG.

Mueller, D. (1986) *Measuring Social Attitudes.* New York: Teachers College Press-Columbia University.

Murphy, R. (1987) *The Body Silent.* New York: Henry Holt and Company.

National Center for Health Statistics in *Science News* v136, August 5, 1989.

Nichols, R. (1990) *The Burning of the Rose*, New York: Fawcett.

Osgood, N. (1985) *Suicide in the Elderly: A Practitioner's Guide to Diagnosis and Mental Health Intervention.* Rockville, MD: Aspen Systems Corp.

Osgood, N., Brant, B. & Lipman, A. (1988) "Patterns of suicidal behavior in long-term care facilities: A preliminary report on an ongoing study." in *Omega—Journal of Death and Dying,* Vol. 19 (1), 1988-89.

Poon, L. (1985) "Difference in Human Memory with Aging: Nature, Causes and Clinical Implications" in *Handbook of the Psychology of Aging.* Birren, J. & Schaie, K. (eds.) New York: Van Nostrand Reinhold Co.

Portwood, D. (1978) *Common-Sense Suicide, The Final Right.* New York: Dodd, Mead.

Reeves, R. (1968) *Minutes of the First Euthanasia Conference,* November 23, 1968.

Rollin, B. (1985) *Last Wish.* New York: Linden Press/Simon & Shuster.

Secouler, L. (1988) "Elderly Suicide Rates Highest in Nation" The CAPsule, Winter 1988.

————(1992) "Our Elders: At High Risk for Humiliation," in the *Journal of Primary Prevention,* Vol. 12, No. 3, 1992.

Secouler, L. & Tronnetti, P. (1989) "Suicide and the Elderly: Assessment and Prevention." *Journal of Osteopathic Medicine,* March: Vol. 3, No. 3.

Seligman, M. (1980) in Zarit, S., *Aging and Mental Disorders,* New York: The Free Press

Supreme Court of the United States, *Rulings re: Assisted Suicide,* June 26, 1997

Tollemache, L. (1873), Fortnightly Review #19.

US Bureau of the Census (1991) *Statistical Abstract of the United States: 1991.* 111th Ed. Washington DC: 1991

US Center for Health Statistics, *No.130. Deaths, by Selected Causes and Selected Characteristics, 1993.* Vital Statistics of the United States, annual.

Veatch, R. (1981) *A Theory of Medical Ethics,* New York: Basic Books.

Zarit, S. (1980) *Aging and Mental Disorders: Psychological Approaches to Assessment and Treatment,* New York: The Free Press.

Index

Ageism, 6, 11, 13, 14
Aging
    for males, 15
    for females, 15, 16
    physiological, 17
    medical model, 47, 58
    psychological concerns, 17, 18,
        29, 39, 42, 46, 59, 61
Alvarez, W. 56, 85
American Geriatrics Society, 65-72,
    85
Ancient Greece & Rome, 21, 22
Aquinas, St. Thomas, 26, 50-51, 85
Aristotle, 22, 85
Atchley, R., 11, 14-15, 17, 85

Baer, L., 29, 54-55, 60, 85
Barrington, M., 57, 85
Batchelor, I., 18, 85
Birren, J., 4, 18, 85
Boswell, J., 5, 86
Bromberg, S., 56-58, 85
Busse, E., 18, 85

Callahan, D., 52-54, 85
Caregiving, 18, 47, 63, 73
Cassell, C., 56-58, 86
Charles., A., 12, 86
Colonial America, 11-13
Comfort, A., 11, 15, 86
Conwell, Y., 4, 86

Christianity, 22, 25, 26, 28, 62, 27,
    55, 62

DeAnfrasio, R., 12, 86
Depression in the elderly, 5, 14, 19,
    20, 36, 38, 42, 44, 55, 57, 58,
    60, 66, 83
Donne, J., 27, 86
Dorpat, T., 5, 86
Durkheim, E., 28, 86

Elder suicide cues, 36, 39, 79, 81
End of life experiences, 59, 66-67
Englehardt, H., 22, 26, 28, 49-51, 87
Erikson, E., 13, 59, 65, 86
Erikson, J. 13, 59, 65, 86
Euthanasia, 27-29, 32, 33, 35, 37-39,
    42, 48, 52, 53, 55, 56, 59-63,
    72, 78
Evans, G., 3, 4, 28, 86

Farberow, N., 3,4, 26-28, 86
Fedden, R., 27, 86
Fischer, D., 11-13, 86
Foregoing of life sustaining
    treatment (FLST), 67
Freud, S., 16, 59, 86

Goffman, E., 15, 19, 32, 86
Gonda, T., 55, 56, 86
Gordon., S., 67, 70, 86